VOICES

Helping Our Children and Youth Listen to Wise Counsel

Rich Griffith

Voices: Helping Our Children and Youth Listen to Wise Counsel
Copyright © 2023 by Rich Griffith
D6 Family Ministry

All rights reserved. No part of this book may be reproduced or transmitted in any form, or by any means, electronic or mechanical, including photocopying or recording, without express written permission from the publisher.

Printed in the United States of America, 2023

ISBN 9781614841647

Unless otherwise stated, all Scripture quotations are from The Holy Bible, New International Version ® NIV ® Copyright © 1973, 1978, 1984, 2011 by Biblica, Inc.

Endorsements

"Before I was adopted, my biological family did not give good input into my life. In fact, the opposite is true. They would have me shoplift or be a lookout during drug deals. Then, I was removed from my family and put into foster care where I started hearing from wise Voices. My dad, Ms. Harriet and church gave me new, and wiser, voices to listen to. Over time, I learned to trust because I discovered adults who are honest with me, who love me, and care about me. I am not perfect but at least I know what it means to listen to wisdom. I am becoming a more confident person."

–Jamie Griffith, Dr. Griffith's son

"When I start counting the blessings of my lifetime the list starts with kids. My own kids and many that keep in touch with me many years later. I've been a teacher, confidant, friend, and guide for many. I realized in my youth how we affect others along our life's path with our energy and time. I'm talking about invested time, not just time spent, but quality time, invested in the precious development of our young people. Building a fun, trusting relationship is a mirrored joy for me. A move to a different state meant I had to leave so much behind, but I was fortunate to find Pastor Rich and learn about his passion to be a guiding light to family development and youth.

Rich confided in me that he had been asked to foster another child. When I offered to help my unmarried pastor, if he needed my help, I hoped he knew how much he could count on me to be there for him and this young boy. And so, the bonding began. Jamie was cautious at first, but I knew we could accomplish so much. I was retired and his mind was so open to finding trust, understanding, and confidence. The trust

VOICES

developed at his own pace, and yes, there were a few lessons learned that were harder than others, but we worked them out, and respect was born between us. And appreciation. And love. At the adoption ceremony I was right along Jamie's side and when Jamie was baptized I became his grand-godmother, a distinction I'm so proud of.

The hours we've spent together have been filled with fun, music, dancing, laughter, work, learning and sharing. I'm honored that I had the opportunity to invest in Jamie. The payoff is tremendous! I'm so proud of the person he has become."

–Harriett Brooke, Jamie's adoptive grand-godmother

"In a day where multiple voices have instant access to our kids, how do we help them discern and listen to the voices that they need to grow and flourish? Dr. Rich Griffith helps us to recognize what impact the cultural voices have on the young, and how we can help them to pay attention to those voices that they need. Timely, vital, and practical, Rich offers us the ability to make a real difference in kids' lives."

–Chap Clark, Ph.D., executive director,
Institute for Ministry Leadership, author,
Hurt 2.0: Inside the World of Today's Teenagers

"In *Voices: Helping Our Children and Youth Listen to Wise Counsel*, you will hear the heart of a father with three adopted teenage sons. You will hear his wide-hearted compassion for the growing number of youth being systemically dropped into the school-to-prison pipeline. You will hear the humble wisdom of a youth-ministry-veteran-turned-professor who has done his homework and now invites us not to give up on the wildly important work of building the kind of constellations of support, nurture, and faith formation that every young person needs."

–Mark DeVries, founder of Ministry Architects
co-founder of Ministry Incubators and author of
Family-Based Youth Ministry and *Sustainable Youth Ministry*.

"As a culture-watcher, I've seen and heard the voices competing for the attention and allegiance of our kids grow in number and volume. In a world calling our kids to 'come and follow' on the wide road that leads to destruction, our kids need to hear and heed those voices that speak the message of the Master—the message that leads to life abundant and life eternal. Rich Griffith helps us know *who* is speaking, *what* they are speaking, and *how we* can best speak Truth with a capital T into the lives of our children and teens. This is a book that will increase your parenting effectiveness!"

–Dr. Walt Mueller, The Center for Parent/Youth Understanding, author, Youth Culture 101, Engaging The Soul of Youth Culture and Track: Navigating Culture: A Student's Guide to Navigating Culture

"What a helpful book! I found Griffiths framing particularly helpful—identification of the various voices influencing our children and youth; and categorizing some as "Big, Quiet Voices" and some as "Small, Loud Voices"—and will be using this in my work."

–Mark Oestreicher, founder, The Youth Cartel, author of numerous books

"In a world full of voices vying for the attention and allegiance of our teens, Dr. Rich Griffith calls for parents and youth workers to become the biggest and most influential of those voices. Rooted in research and Scripture, each chapter includes practical discussion guides for teaching teenagers to discern the message and intent of the many voices they hear."

–Lee Barnett, D.Min., Ph.D., vice provost for student affairs, continuing education, and strategic academic partnerships at Columbia Southern University, co-author, Ministry with Youth in Crisis, 2nd Ed.

VOICES

"In this excellent resource, Rich Griffith reimagines parenting and ministry as the art of helping children and youth discern the numerous voices in their lives and develop their own voice along the way. This brilliant approach provides a unique perspective for parents and children/youth leaders alike. Filled with thought provoking questions *Voices* provides space for critical reflection on the noise filled culture that continually encircles our lives today."

–Mark Cannister, Ed. D., professor of Christian Ministries, Gordon College, author, *Teenagers Matter: Making Student Ministry a Priority in the Church (Youth, Family, and Culture* series).

"'Careful the things you say, children will listen,' sang the Witch in the Broadway musical, *Into the Woods*. Children and youth do listen, but who are they listening to? In Rich Griffith's book, *Voices: Helping Our Children and Youth Listen to Wise Counsel*, parents and all who spend time with children and youth will learn a lot about who kids are listening to these days and why. Adults will also learn their voices matter, and Griffith shows us how to cut through the noise of the competing voices and speak so our children and youth will listen."

–Dr. Robb Redman, Ph.D., professor and director of Ministry Programs, South College, director, Worship Leader Institute

"This practical and clear call to pay attention to our teens is much needed. Teens are listening to many voices. Dr. Griffith helps us engage our teens and the voices that vie for their attention. Lively stories are mixed with biblical insight, research, and true wisdom that parents and those who care for teens should hear and heed."

–Mike Severe, Ph.D., professor of Christian Ministries, Taylor University, co-author, *Ministry with Youth in Crisis, revised edition*

"Are you worried that God's voice is being drowned out among our children and youth? How can the next generation hear God above the clamor of all the loud, competing noises in our world? My friend, Rich Griffith, has written a practical resource that offers parents and grandparents practical hope in the midst of worry. Rich reminds us that God is not panicking about the next generation. With seasoned wisdom, Rich wants to help you equip your kids to discern and pursue God's plans."

–Dr. Ken Castor, family & NextGen pastor, Wooddale Church, author of *Make a Difference: 365 World-Changing Devotions* and *Grow Down: How to Build a Jesus-Centered Faith*

"Our kids are being discipled by multiple voices, and everybody is fighting for their voice to be the loudest. Who will win the ear of the next generations? Dr. Rich Griffith expertly exposes the folly of loud, cultural voices that feed our kids lies that never satisfy while encouraging the steady, wise voices of parents, mentors, and Truth. With insightful wisdom and practical tools, *Voices* is a must-have resource for parents and practitioners who desire to help kids discern those softer and wiser voices above the din of the noise around them."

–JJ Jones, M.Div., D.Min., pastor of groups, Fellowship Bible Church, Nashville Tennessee; adjunct professor, youth ministries, Toccoa Falls College

"I have had the privilege of knowing Dr. Griffith when I was a middle school student and now as an adult with teenage children of my own. He has always been a positive Voice to me and my family throughout the years. I could always reach out to him as a young person seeking wise advice on the struggles we all experience while growing up in middle school and high school. It is so nice to still have that Voice of reason while my wife and I are raising our own teenagers. Now we are having conversations on how to best raise our children in a Christian way and be the louder Voice over all the other voices vying for our children's attention. This book will allow everyone access to the wisdom that Dr. Griffith has that I have been blessed to experience for the last 25+ years. He has

VOICES

been, and continues to make, a huge impact on my life and indirectly the lives of my children and other students that God places in my life. I hope you are blessed as much as I am."

–David Dutton, life-long friend, volunteer youth leader, former youth group member, parent of teens

Table of Contents

Chapter 1: Listening to the Right Voices 1
Why Are Voices Important?
Filtering the Voices With the Three Ts
Time
Transparency
Trust

Chapter 2: Big, Quiet Voices 17
The Voice of Parents and Grandparents
The Voice of Mentors
The Voice of the Church
The Voice of Diversity
The Voice of God

Chapter 3: Small, Loud Voices 65
The Voice of Peers
The Voice of Consumerism
The Voice of (Social) Media
The Voice of Culture

VOICES

Chapter 4: Helping Youth Find and Use Their Own Voice **107**

Ways to Discover Your Voice

Appendix: Ways to Disciple Your Children "As You Go" **119**

At Home

In Church and Your Community

Introduction

Big, Quiet Voices or Small, Loud Voices

Children and youth are being bombarded with competing voices in their lives. Some of these voices are helpful while others are dysfunctional and damaging. Institutions that are supposed to care for the healthy development of young people are vying for the attention and affection of our children in pursuit of their own adult-driven agendas and worldview. This has caused a significant amount of loneliness, anxiety, depression, and dysconnectivity in our children and youth. Child psychologists, such as Dr. David Elkind and others, have warned of this danger.[1]

Multiple sources report that Gen Z is the loneliest generation.[2] It seems as though the more we have tried to focus on youth, the more difficult it has become to raise healthy young people. This book was written to help parents,

---

[1] Clark, Chap. *Hurt 2.0: Inside the World of Today's Teenagers*. Baker Academic, 2011.

[2] https://www.google.com/search?q=Gen+Z+is+the+loneliest+generation

grandparents who are "re-parenting," youth workers, teachers—and others who have a heart to help hurting young people—find the causes of this loneliness and anxiety and gain practical counsel to combat the hurt that young people experience.

There are nefarious forces that do not have the well-being of our youth and children in mind! The proliferation of online pornography, hypersexualized children in *entertainment*, a lack of digital media monitoring or accountability, the destabilization of the family, growing "do what you will" secularization void of a moral code and so many other actors are easy seductions for our young.

An older minister made a comical but profound observation. He said, "Have you ever noticed that the loudest noise comes from the shallow end of the pool?" His imagery pointed out a deep truth. As I recalled my experience of being a lifeguard when I was younger, his comment rang true. I remember that the loudest noise came from the shallow end of the pool. The minister was calling attention to the people who stir up controversy and contribute a lot of noise.

Our world can be like that pool. It is as if there are too many *voices* screaming into the lives of our young people. Sadly, many of these *voices* are hindering the process of young people discovering their own voice. Immature people want to play and please themselves. They do *a lot* of talking and love to put themselves first and hear themselves talk. In fact, they think everyone should see life their way. Mature people are not like that. Mature people are willing to listen to others and even respectfully disagree with them when necessary.

This book is about those different voices. It is about teenagers and the voices they listen to. There are a lot of voices trying to speak into the life of teenagers. Some are mature voices that care about teenagers. Others are immature and only care about what they want and use teenagers to meet their desires. The more mature voices are the big, quiet voices. The immature voices tend to be the small, loud voices—the voices at the shallow end of the pool. I hope this book will help you and your child discover how to listen to the right voices and why that is so important.

Chapter 1
Listening to the Right Voices

Why Are Voices Important?

Voices have influence. Voices help us determine direction in our lives. Voices can be helpful or harmful. We are constantly surrounded by voices. Of all the voices we hear, how do we determine which are the most helpful and important voices to listen to? An ancient story that still rings true today offers insight. In 1 Kings 19:9b–13 we read about the prophet Elijah.

> And the word of the Lord came to him: "What are you doing here, Elijah?" He replied, "I have been very zealous for the Lord God Almighty. The Israelites have rejected your covenant, torn down your altars, and put your prophets to death with the sword. I am the only one left, and now they are trying to kill me too." The Lord said, "Go out and stand on the mountain in the presence of the Lord, for the Lord is about to pass by." Then a great and powerful wind tore the mountains apart and shattered the rocks before the Lord,

VOICES

but the LORD** was not in the wind. After the wind there was an earthquake, but the L**ORD** was not in the earthquake. After the earthquake came a fire, but the L**ORD** was not in the fire. And after the fire came a gentle whisper. When Elijah heard it, he pulled his cloak over his face and went out and stood at the mouth of the cave.**

Of all the chaos, earth-shaking, and awe-inspiring things to happen, how strange is it that God's voice was found in a whisper? Also, it seems like a strange question for God to ask Elijah, "What are you doing here?" After all, isn't God omniscient (all-knowing), omnipotent (all-powerful), and omnipresent (all-present)? It is not the first time God asked the question. Why would God ask this question? The question is not to give God an answer. It's a rhetorical question to help Elijah wrestle with where he currently finds himself.

To set the stage, Elijah, the prophet of God, lived in a time when there were many loud-mouthed and arrogant people. These were people who wanted to do whatever pleased them. They ignored God and even mocked Him. The people of Israel were led by a king named Ahab and a queen named Jezebel. When you read about the wicked leaders, Ahab and Jezebel, you will discover they were the most loud-mouthed and arrogant of them all. So, if the leaders of a nation are loud-mouthed and arrogant, it is easy to see how the nation would take their lead! Both Ahab and Jezebel not only lacked maturity and wisdom, but they were also incredibly selfish and used (and killed) people to get what they wanted! Whose voice does it seem it would be better to listen to: the voices of Ahab and Jezebel or the voice of God?

Elijah was a man that God had called to speak the truth against Ahab, Jezebel, and the nation of Israel. Can you imagine having the rulers *and* the people of a nation against you? Needless to say, there were a lot of loud-mouthed, selfish, arrogant, and destructive people out to get Elijah. Elijah had a major encounter against all the evil voices around him and he won the contest because God was with him (you can read about this in 1 Kings 18). It was an incredible encounter, however, even though Elijah listened to the voice of God and had a great victory, Jezebel threatened to kill Elijah. Elijah felt like he was on his own and all alone. He felt abandoned and was so depressed, he wanted to die. Have you ever wondered why it seems like the *good guys* who do what is right are the ones who suffer the most while the *bad guys* seem to get away with murder? (Ahab and Jezebel tried to get away with murder and, by all accounts of *worldly standards*, they were prospering.) However, God was not finished with Elijah! (God wasn't finished with Ahab or Jezebel either and their wicked deeds caught up with them.)

It is important to notice God was not in the huge destructive wind (verse 11b). God was not in the earthquake (verse 11c). God was not in the fire (verse 12a), but God was in the whisper (12b). So many times, people want to know how they can hear from God. Often, people look for God to move in extraordinary ways. The fact of the matter is, God often speaks in the *boring day-to-day* and in the still small voice we *hear* inside of us. The main point is that God often speaks to us through a whisper in our souls. He often speaks to us through other people who are not as loud as the noise of the world, and these are the people who have a godly character we can trust. Here is the question: How in the world can we hear the

VOICES

whisper of God when the world around us is always loud and noisy? This question will be answered in the following pages.

As a teenager grows up it's important to learn how to drive, get good grades, do well in extracurricular activities, graduate high school, get a job, or attend college. But of far greater importance is for a teenager to discover who he or she is. This is called, "identity formation" and it is exactly what it sounds like. In fact, identity formation is the primary task of adolescence. As a person matures, the circle of voices he or she hears grows. As the number of voices increases, it takes wisdom to drown out the voices that are not helpful. With the proliferation of social media, those voices have only increased in number with a dizzying effect.

The first voices a baby hears are the parents—even while in the womb. These first voices are the most significant voices a baby hears. The more you can trust those healthy voices and listen to them, the more mature and healthier a young person becomes. That babies can begin learning to trust a parent's voice can be attested to in the works of psychologists Erik Erikson, Lawrence Kohlberg, and Jean Piaget (among others).

We need to remember some significant details about the creation account in Genesis. First of all, humans were created for community. This, of course, requires being in relationship with each other. It is interesting to note that, even though Adam was in a perfectly good relationship with God, God said, "It is not good for the man to be alone. I will make a helper suitable for him" (Genesis 2:18). This may sound surprising, since we often hear it said God is all we need, right? Well, yes and no. Yes, "For in him we live and move and have our being" (Acts 17:28), we need God to sustain us, but we also need the companionship of other people. Notice, when God said it was not good for man to be alone, that was *before* the Fall of humanity.

God created humanity for relationships and placed them in the Garden of Eden. They enjoyed perfect relationship with God and each other, then, the other voice spoke to them. Tragically, they didn't listen to the right voice.

It's a familiar story. Satan came in the garden and tempted Adam and Eve with a fruit of a different kind. We can read about this small, loud voice:

> **Now the serpent was more crafty than any of the wild animals the L**ord **God had made. He said to the woman, "Did God really say, 'You must not eat from any tree in the garden'?" The woman said to the serpent, "We may eat fruit from the trees in the garden, but God did say, 'You must not eat fruit from the tree that is in the middle of the garden, and you must not touch it, or you will die.'"**
>
> **"You will not certainly die," the serpent said to the woman. "For God knows that when you eat from it your eyes will be opened, and you will be like God, knowing good and evil"** (Genesis 3:1–5).

Notice how Satan asked first, "Did God really say...?" The first indicator of an unhealthy voice is that it gets you to question what the good voice has said. Eve answered back about what God did say, but Satan continued in his quest to separate Adam and Eve from God. He made Eve doubt God's word and further, appealed to vanity—to be like God. Now, this is tricky. We often look at Eve and, with our 20/20 hindsight vision, want to scream, "Eve, don't do it! It's a trap!" Notice how crafty the serpent is. We might think being "like God" would be good. Yet, in an effort to "be like God," there is a fatal flaw in thinking we could ever be like Him in position, authority, or knowledge. Further, Satan said they would know, "good and evil." Notice Satan did not say, they would know "*the difference between* good and evil." In fact, in the next generation, with Cain and Abel Adam and Eve would *know* the most sinister evil when Cain killed Abel! This is what happens when we listen to the wrong voices. Yes, we pay a price, but how much more of a price is paid by the following generations? It is easy to see that the voices we listen to are incredibly important!

As more voices enter our world, we must determine who is worth listening to and who is not. Through your reading of this book, I hope young and old are encouraged to find the right voices and filter through the many voices that seek to be heard. The right voices can help build a solid foundation for a fruitful life. In the diagrams below, you see a representation of the different voices in a typical teen's life.

The Many Voices in a Teen's Life

- Family
- Teachers
- Church/Youth Pastor
- Work
- Social Media A "biggee" that overlaps with friends.
- School
- Peers
- Coach Sports
- Boyfriend Girlfriend
- Self Perspective

- Teens have a significant number of voices vying for their attention—all with different worldviews.
- Trying to manage communication with so many voices creates many different "selves."
- It takes wisdom to discern the different voices.

Teens hear these voices every day. Some are more important than others. Some are "louder" than others. Teens must navigate how they communicate with the different voices around them. For instance, teens have different types of conversations with their friends than they do with their parents. Teens interact differently with their teachers than they do their youth pastor. They are trying to make sense of all the voices—especially as some of them might contradict each other as shown below.

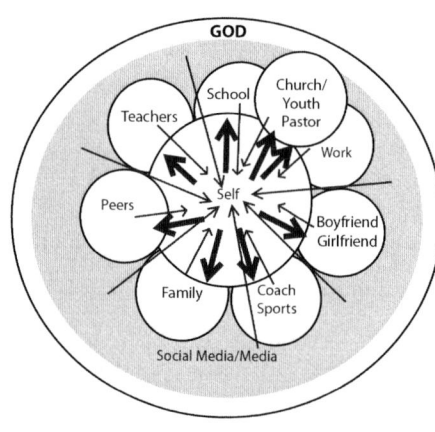

- Since a primary task of becoming an adult is "Identity Formation," we must question, "How do our children interact with all these voices, choose the wise ones, and minimize the poor ones?
- How does environment, relationships, identity, faith, and a variety of influences help shape our children's worldview?
- While we hope the church will be a significant positive influence, this cannot be assumed in an increasingly secular culture.

Communication with God is not included in this illustration since the voices young people hear often determine their worldview about God and where He fits. However, I will write on how we can help our young people hear from God. Unfortunately, attending church is not a high priority for many people today—young or old. Covid-19 has shown us how the church has become an accessory in many lifestyles rather than an essential element of spiritual growth, because many of the other voices (social media, news, peers, schools, etc.) paint a very negative view of all churches. When we listen to the voices of the secular culture, combined with our own inner voice that may remind us of bad experiences by church leaders, it is easy to stop going to church. Sure, there are bad churches, but most churches are filled with people who love God and want to help people.

With all these different voices going back and forth, it is no wonder we can sometimes feel anxiety! How can Gen Z, the most digitally connected generation, be "the loneliest generation"? One theory is that being overly connected to multiple, non-caring digital voices creates the loneliness. What is worse, in times past many of these voices would communicate with each other to help young people feel valued and grow up in a healthy way. Churches and schools used to collaborate with each other. Parents and schools used to communicate much more with each other. Now, unfortunately, many of these organizations not only do not communicate with each other but they also have different values that conflict with each other. No wonder there is so much confusion in our society and for our young!

Young people get their values from the voices they hear. When they are younger—before identity formation—they often parrot back what they think the various voices *want* them to say. So even if values and moral standards conflict, children and early adolescents will simply say back what they think the authority wants them to say. Values are incredibly important in life. Morals are a part of the formation of values. A person's worldview often determines their morals and values. A person's worldview is how one sees and interacts with the world. What happens when a teen gets a certain type of moral message from parents but another type from their school and yet another type from their friends? Contradicting voices cause confusion and make decision making very complex and difficult. Again, no wonder there is a lot of anxiety among teens and their peers! Processing the messages between conflicting voices can cause anxiety.

We all know that societies and cultures change. When Nations were more "agrarian" (lots of farms before the industrial revolution), there were fewer "voices" to compete for our attention. Families were typically larger and extended. Farms needed a lot of children to work the farm. The primary voices children and youth listened to were parents, church leaders and schoolteachers. It was good that the messages children and youth received were pretty much the same. The not-so-good was the lack of diversity in those voices. Fast forward to today and now there are a lot more voices that speak into the lives of children and youth. Sometimes this is good and sometimes it is destructive. We must teach our children to be wise and reject the voices that lack your family's morality, values, and worldview.

The Post-Modern culture will say, "There is not any one truth but many truths." This can cause a great deal of confusion. Friends, media, and schools may say, "Pre-marital sex is okay (or even good for you)," but parents, church, and a youth pastor say, "Pre-marital sex can be harmful to you in the long-run." Who is a teen going to believe? It depends on who takes the time to gain the ears and heart of the teen! Sometimes, we pick the voice we *want* to hear even if we know it is wrong. While culture says, "Pre-marital sex is normal," God's Word teaches that sex outside of marriage is a destructive sin. Even academic studies and research shows that young people can be set back academically, emotionally, and financially, depending upon the consequences of engaging in pre-marital sex.

Sometimes, it may not be about *right or wrong*. In those situations, the better question might be, "Is this a wise decision?"

VOICES

At some point our young people are going to choose the voices to which they listen. Our goal is to help them choose the wise voices. This takes a great deal of wisdom as well as investments of time, emotional energy, and meaningful interactions.

The Apostle Paul wrote about maturity that comes about by knowing Christ and wisdom. He writes in Ephesians 4:14–16,

> **Then we will no longer be infants, tossed back and forth by the waves, and blown here and there by every wind of teaching and by the cunning and craftiness of people in their deceitful scheming. Instead, speaking the truth in love, we will grow to become in every respect the mature body of him who is the head, that is, Christ. From him the whole body, joined and held together by every supporting ligament, grows and builds itself up in love, as each part does its work.**

Maturity is knowing which voices to choose that are going to help you grow into a person who has a fruitful, gratifying, and productive life.

One final thing: In our Western culture, especially in America, we hear all the time that the parent's *job* is to raise children to become healthy independent young adults. The problem with this thinking is that sometimes we raise them to be too independent. When this happens, we forget that our actions impact each other. On the one extreme, there is co-dependency. We have seen this with *helicopter parents* who hover over their kids to *make sure they succeed* (when in fact it is the parents succeeding through their kids). Have you heard of the recently published term *bulldozer parent*? This is a parent who clears any obstacles or challenges out of their child's path. This is dangerous because kids become co-dependent on others for their success. Unhealthy independence is the same thing but on the other side of the spectrum. Instead, we should be raising our children to understand that we are *interdependent*. Our relationships and decisions impact our lives and the lives of many others. Teaching healthy interdependence helps a young person discover their identity through healthy relationships and having positive voices in their lives.

Filtering the Voices With the Three Ts

There are three significant contributors to knowing which voices to trust in life. They are time, transparency, and trust—in that order. I want to offer these *three Ts* as filters for helping young people determine which voices to listen to. These three filters are interdependent. It is difficult to build trust with someone has not invested time in your life and is not transparent with you. If someone tries to build trust too quickly without putting time into the relationship, that should be a warning! When someone you do not know says, "Trust me," we should exercise caution. We cannot know someone's intentions and whether we can trust that person until we have spent time getting to know them. If someone is very guarded and not transparent with their words and actions, it is difficult to trust that seemingly secretive person. We will discuss each of these filters for knowing which voices to listen to.

Time

Children are becoming the victims of a lack of time spent in meaningful conversations with parents. Research states that parents spend as little as five to ten minutes per day in meaningful conversation with their children. Not surprisingly, dads tend to spend less time than moms in meaningful conversation with their children. Some research indicates that parents are spending less and less time with children in both developmental (playing, teaching, reading, talking) and non-developmental (basic care, household management) engagements. Much of this also has to do with family makeup. It is more challenging, for instance, for a single parent to spend quality time in both developmental and non-developmental engagements due to work and home-life responsibilities (Fallesen & Gähler, 2020). Other research states worldwide that parents are spending more time with their children (Ortiz-Ospina, 2020). What all the research seems to indicate is that parents who come from backgrounds with higher education (college or graduate school), who offer consistency and structure in the home, and who spend significant time with their children, have children who are healthier and happier than homes that do not provide these things.

Teenagers contemplate and discuss among themselves which voices have earned the right to be heard. Jim Rayburn, the founder of the ministry Young Life coined the phrase, "earning the right to be heard." Deep, meaningful, and trusting relationships can only happen over time. Time is the element that allows one person to get to know the character of another person. Authentic and intimate relationships also take time to develop. While some would claim, "Love at first sight," the reality is love is a commitment that goes beyond first sight to go through the good times and the bad times.

Transparency

Unfortunately, we live in a society where charisma often trumps character. Unfortunately, many people who are attractive, speak well, yield influence, and display charisma, but lack character, are often the people who find themselves engaging in unethical or immoral behaviors. A charismatic person who lacks character can be a great manipulator. It is only through spending time with a person that you begin to see their true character. People who lack character also lack transparency.

My friend and colleague, Dr. Russell Huizing, makes some great observations about *character, crisis,* and *transparency.* The reason we can trust our family members is not that life is perfect together, rather we have a deep relationship with our family because, when we argued and fought, we still stay together. The moments of life that do not go well—or go the way we want them—are where character is formed. A *crisis* can show us our weaknesses that we might need to work on. This is exactly when we need wise voices. The people you love the most are the people you went through the tough times together and yet they remained committed as family or friends. Anyone can be a fair-weather friend: a person who sticks with you only when things are going well. Proverbs 27:6 says, "Wounds from a friend can be trusted, but an enemy multiplies kisses." This simple truth means that sometimes a friend will tell you the hard things you don't want to hear, but someone who is a fair-weather friend will manipulate you with flattery and compliments just so they can get you to do something for them.

VOICES

Someone who is only looking out for themselves all the time is not the kind of friend we want!

Getting to know someone's true *character* can only happen over time when things are going well or poorly. If you are part of a team, you can see who has good character and who does not. If the team is doing poorly and a player wants to place blame on everyone and everything else, rather than considering how that individual player can improve, that player lacks character. A leader always asks the question, "How can I improve?" first and then, "How can we as a team improve?" Good character is developed over time and through trials—which can be seen as crisis. Good character doesn't blame, good character finds solutions. A person with even better character is someone who is willing to lift up the other person. Philippians 2:3–4 says, "Do nothing out of selfish ambition or vain conceit. Rather, in humility value others above yourselves, not looking to your own interests but each of you to the interests of the others." This is not a popular message with the world, but remember, the most noise comes from the shallow end of the pool and it is usually the people in the shallow end of the pool who do not go deep in life. Another important thing to remember about character can be found in 1 Corinthians 15:33. This verse could be a key verse for this whole book: "Do not be misled: 'Bad company corrupts good character.'"

Have you ever known someone who seems to have something to hide? They don't seem very trustworthy, do they? When I worked in a home for troubled adolescents, unhealthy secrecy seemed to be something that bred dysfunction. We all know a little bit about this. If we have done something wrong, we tend to want to hide it. In fact, depending upon the level of guilt, shame, or fear, we will lie and deny having done anything wrong for fear of consequences. On the other hand, other people might have done some bad things to us and either *swore us to secrecy* or threatened to harm us or others if we told anyone. Secrecy is the opposite of transparency. To build trust with someone, they should not hold secrets from you or encourage you to keep secrets. Even professional counselors do not keep secrets. They do hold information confidential, but this means they are working with someone who needs to get things off their chest. Professional counselors are required to tell the proper authorities if someone is going to harm themselves or someone else. They cannot *keep a secret* when it comes to something like this. If someone is going to hurt themselves or someone else, the counselor must be transparent in order to get the person the help they need. There is a difference in confidentiality and secrecy.

In my own life, as well as the lives of my sons, I have given permission to our mentors to "keep a confidence, but not hold secrets." This is an important distinction. Unhealthy people, who do unhealthy things, often do them in secret. People who are healthy build transparent relationships with others who will hold confidence, but not secrets. Here is what I mean by this: If I were struggling with pornography, my mentor would hold this in confidence. He would not want to embarrass me, so they do not tell anyone. But he would hold me accountable in my attempts to overcome this addictive behavior. However, if I tell my mentor that I am going to commit suicide, I want my mentor to tell the right people so I can get the help I need! When crisis comes, transparency is essential to becoming or staying healthy.

Trust

Trust is earned and built by time and transparency. It does not always come easy and when it is broken, it is very difficult to earn back trust. In Exodus 18:21, Moses was given advice from his father-in-law, Jethro, on how to delegate and choose leaders. The primary qualifications for leadership were to be capable "men who fear God, trustworthy men who hate dishonest gain." Trustworthy people are also honest people. You probably know someone who lies so much they are known as a liar and is simply not trustworthy. A person who lies should not be a trusted voice. In fact, the Bible strongly states that (unrepentant) liars will not be in Heaven (1 Timothy 1:10; Revelation 21:8).

Chapter 2
Big, Quiet Voices

The Voice of Parents and Grandparents

First, let's acknowledge that our culture has drastically changed. Much of these changes were driven by technology. This section has an emphasis on parents and grandparents. There are an increasing number of grandparents who are "re-parenting" their grandchildren. Also, families have been ever increasingly moving from *traditional* (nuclear) families to *non-traditional* (permeable) families. In other words, family structures are becoming much more diverse—something traditional churches may be slow to recognize and plan for.

Secondly, let me be very real and transparent: As mentioned, I have spent many years in ministry as a youth pastor, pastor, and ministry leader and yet, when I finally became a parent, I had very little clue on how to disciple my own children! For me, discipleship was something the church did. I was a part of making disciples as a youth pastor and a pastor. It was part of my job and I was willing to partner with parents—when parents were willing—which seemed to me to be very rare. Most parents probably thought, "This is why the church pays a youth pastor. It is his (or her) job to disciple my kid." The truth of the matter is that, while I had a successful youth ministry, and while we were involved in outreach and discipleship, I cannot be sure how many young people stuck with their faith into adulthood. For many of those students, youth group was full of great memories, but I have no idea how many of those young people are still walking with Jesus in life-impacting ways. The current statistics state anywhere from 59–75 percent of young people who grew up in church leave the church. They report remaining "spiritual," but not necessarily "Christian" (McDowell, 2018). The book *Soul Searching: The Religious and Spiritual Lives of American Teenagers* (2005) brings a significant amount of research on the lives of teens and young adults. Only about 10 percent of young adults are attending a weekly worship service and other opportunity for spiritual growth (Smith and Denton, p. 141).

It is sad to think about the amount of money spent on youth ministry (staff, curriculum, resources, events, trips, conferences, etc.) to have so many young people leaving the church. I started this section with a confession as a parent and as a seemingly failed youth pastor because I discovered, like most parents, we have made discipleship far too difficult and we have resorted to hiring a professional. I can't name a single parent that ever bought a discipleship-based curriculum to use in their home with their children. Even as a youth pastor, I had a difficult time finding solid discipleship material that lasted beyond being a fad! Frankly, this is why I felt led to write this book on voices. The most important voice in faith development still belongs to parents. Yet, how can a parent disciple their children when they are not trained to do so? Often, parents are engaged in small groups, Sunday School, worship, and other church activities, but how can they translate that into discipling their own children? With this in mind, I offer a few suggestions:

1. You don't have to have a degree from a seminary to disciple your child! The fact that we have professionalized youth discipleship has been a contributing factor as to why youth walk away from their faith. Parents have more of an impact on a child's faith development than some program at church.

2. Partner with your youth pastor! Even though many teens don't want their parents hanging out with the youth group, you can find ways to be involved in your church's youth ministry. Find out what your kids are discussing in youth group or other venues at church. Parents make the best youth ministry partners. If every parent of a teen dismissed the idea of being involved in youth group, most youth groups would be at a severe disadvantage of not having voices of wisdom and empathy.

3. There are great resources available to you as a parent that are often very affordable. (I am not recommending the following resources just because D6 Family Ministry is the publisher of this book. Quite frankly, I have found that D6 Family has a significant amount of helpful and affordable resources for helping parents raise godly children and youth (www.D6family.org). For instance, one of the discipleship approaches I have used with my youngest son, Jamie, is a book by Dr. Ron Hunter called, *About Me, About You: Generational Legacy Journal*. This book is full of great "get-to-know-you-better" conversation starters. I have used this book as a launching point for spiritual conversations. By engaging in this book and spending time with my son, I am also being transparent and building trust.

4. Read Scripture and talk about it. One of the things that scares parents is the fear that their child may know more than he or she does. A simple solution to this fear is to say, "That is a great question. I don't know the answer, but let's find out together!" Being transparent will build trust and leads to further conversations.

5. Reclaim the family table. Mark Glanville writes, "Jesus ate his way through the Gospels" (Glanville, 2012). Having a meal together is not just about food, it is about connecting in relationships, meeting physical needs, and having time of nurturing both body and soul. This is another simple approach to discipleship: engaging in something that you do every day with intentionality!

6. Stop the busyness—this includes digital engagement. We talk to our kids about drugs, smoking, alcohol, and sex as risky behaviors but we must catch up on our conversations about digital media consumption as risky and addictive behavior as well. We have heard it said, "Idle hands are the devil's workshop" but this pop-culture theology has wrecked families! We have stressed out ourselves and our children by keeping them super busy. If God speaks in a whisper, how do we expect to hear from Him if our lives are full of noise and busyness? Busyness is also the very enemy that keeps us as parents from having meaningful conversations with our children! It takes time to listen and to be heard! Unfortunately, most of our conversations with our children are rushed unless there is a point of crisis. Having meaningful, and even fun, conversations help us to avoid crisis (or at least helps take the sting a bit more out of the crisis).

7. Use life as discipleship. The whole premise of Deuteronomy 6:4–9 is to have conversations about life and spirituality "as you go." Life is your greatest discipleship tool. This is why it is important to spend quality time in spiritual conversations with your children. Think of how many conversations get missed due to busyness and the frantic pace of life. Over forty years ago, Dr. David Elkind warned of the dangers of children growing up too fast and too soon (*The Hurried Child*, 1981). Dr. Robert Kegan agrees that our culture is not only forcing children to grow up too soon, rather we are stealing childhood away from our children due to the fact that children are getting caught in cycles of self-preservation and self-promotion (Kegan, 1994, p. 4). Realize, this was written before social media! Mark DeVries writes, "Our culture has put an incredible emotional weight on the shoulders of the nuclear family, a weight that I believe God never intended for families to bear alone" (DeVries, 2004, p. 17). I echo these sentiments and would definitely expand this sentiment to non-traditional families! The question must be asked, "Is anyone listening?"

8. Practice Sabbath together. The antidote to busyness is rest. Sabbath also includes play! Having common, fun, and shared experiences not only expands your time together, but it also expands transparency and trust!

Could it be the very reason there is a debate between "emerging adult" or "extended adolescence" is because our young people have grown up without a carefree childhood, a childhood where they were nurtured, protected, or mentored? Is it possible that young adults are trying to reclaim what they missed when they were younger and now they are labeled *irresponsible*? Maybe they are irresponsible because, as adults, we did not do the responsible things we needed to do to truly nurture them. After all, wouldn't this be the very definition of systemic abandonment or systemic isolation?

As I have continued to ponder the question, "How can I disciple my children in ways that are authentic and meaningful?" I truly had to wrestle with this. To be further helpful, I have included some ideas on easy ways to disciple your children. The article is entitled, "Ways to Disciple Your Children 'As You Go'" (Appendix).

The first voice your baby hears is mom and dad's voices. You have probably seen movies or heard that a pre-born baby can hear his or her parent's voice. A baby can hear his or her mother's heartbeat and in later development hear sounds outside of her body. It's not uncommon for people to sing to their unborn babies. Parents should never discount what their baby can hear while still in the womb. If parents are healthy, nurturing, and prioritize the child's needs, deep trust is developed by the child. Erikson said that the very first stage a child goes through is "Trust versus Mistrust" (Erikson, 1950). If a child is raised in a trusting and nurturing home, the child has better odds to develop and grow in very healthy ways (the fruitful life). If a child grows up in an environment where the child's needs are not met and trust is not established, odds are that the child will not grow and develop in very healthy ways.

When I first left the Army and started college, I worked in a home for youth who needed to know how to reconnect with their parents in meaningful ways. During that time, I learned that children often get their first impressions about God from their interactions with their parents. If the parents were loving, nurturing, patient, kind, and trustworthy, this is how children often saw God. If, however, parents were unloving, selfish, impatient, cruel, and untrustworthy, then children often believe this is the character and nature of God. If a parent (or parents) were present and involved with the child, the child saw God as present, but if the parents were aloof and withheld affection, this is how children also perceived God.

When I am teaching or writing about the things of God, I like to usually start with God, but in this case, I felt like it was important to start with parents since this is where children get their first impression of God. With this in mind, we need to say some honest things about parents. These are things parents may not feel comfortable saying to their children.

I have discovered that when parents mess up, they may not be willing to admit they made a mistake. There are a couple of reasons for this. First, as parents we do not want to lose the feeling of being the expert in our child's life. We want our children to trust what we tell them. Some children who have great parents can see their parents as something like *superheroes*. We are afraid that our children can often be very disappointed when they realize we are not perfect. The other reason for parents not admitting they make mistakes is that we are trying to do the best we can as parents. There is no real manual written on child raising and, even if there were, every child is different. What might work for one child might not work for another child in the same home and family.

Parents are reluctant to admit they make mistakes because they are afraid their children will hold their mistakes against them. Honestly, some children do use the mistakes of their parents against their parents. However, I remind you that Adam and Eve had God as their Father—a perfect Father—

and yet they chose to rebel against Him. Another reason parents may not own up to their mistakes is that we just don't like being wrong! However, admitting when we are wrong or apologizing is a deeply humbling experience and yet, when done authentically, it builds that sense of transparency. Further, it allows our children to see that they can make mistakes, own up to them, learn from them, and move on.

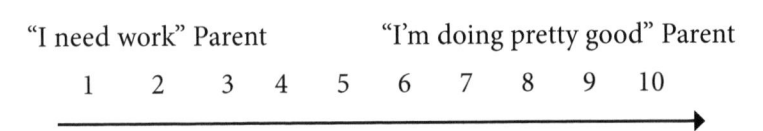

"I need work" Parent   "I'm doing pretty good" Parent
    1   2   3   4   5   6   7   8   9   10
⟶

Frankly, there are parents all along the spectrum between "bad" and "excellent" parents. Let's assume that you rate yourself a 9. (It is pretty much impossible to be a 10 because no one is perfect except God.) Where would you rate yourself in the areas of time, transparency, and trust? Where would your children rate you?

Time Rating *(I spend a meaningful amount of time (20 to 30 minutes) per day with my children every day, including prayer, active listening, and asking open-ended questions)*: _____

Transparency Rating *(I admit to my mistakes, apologize, ask for forgiveness, and don't hold secrets)*: _____

Trust Rating *(I keep my word and can be trusted in all things with my child)*: _____

How did you do? How do you think your children would rate you?

Questions

1. **Time:** As a parent, how are you intentionally taking time to be a discipling voice in your child's life? How much time each day do you spend talking to your child about the things of God, Jesus, the Kingdom of God, etc.? How could you improve this?
2. **Transparency:** When you make mistakes, are you willing to apologize and make amends?
3. **Trust:** Is there anything that keeps you from being the spiritual leader for your children? How can you overcome these challenges?
4. What are all the busy challenges in your family's life that keep you from connecting with each other? What could you or members of your family give up?
5. What regular and intentional time(s) do you have planned throughout each week that allows you to connect with each other?

Conversations With Your Children

- Do you feel like we are often too busy? If so, how can we become less busy?
- Do you feel like I spend enough meaningful time with you? Do you think I really listen to what is going on in your life?
- What is your best memory of us spending time together? What makes that such a great memory?
- If you could plan a day just to hang out and have fun, what would you want to do?

VOICES

The Voice of Mentors

The positive influence a mentor can have on the life of a child and teen who are moving into young adulthood cannot be overstated! Even young people who have suffered through trauma, abuse, and other risk-factors have benefitted from a mentor. In my doctoral work, I was able to show how our young people are being criminalized by the various systems that are supposed to nurture them. While this may be the case, there is also a significant number of studies that show even children and youth who are considered "at risk" and come from traumatic backgrounds can have positive futures when mentored by at least one caring adult.

As an adoptive parent of kids who came from at-risk backgrounds, I sought and found mentors for my sons because I knew I could not be the only voice in my kids' lives. My sons' mentors shared our values and worldview, but also provided a proper amount of healthy diversity. Too many diverse voices without the same values and worldview can create a great deal of confusion rather than clarity that helps a teen in their identity formation. More diverse voices are appropriate after a young person matures and finds stability and security in their identity and faith development. I do not want my children to simply reflect me. I want them to reflect God and who He is helping them to become.

My sons have had mentors like Mr. Darryl, Mr. Keith, L. J., Ms. Harriett, and others. These friends have been wonderful mentors in the lives of my sons. For now, I want to tell you about Ms. Harriett because she is the latest mentor my son and I have interacted with. I know I am not supposed to ever ask a woman's age but Ms. Harriett is older than me. Having sons, most of their mentors have been men—except for L. J. and Ms. Harriett. Ms. Harriett is Jamie's mentor. At the time of this writing, he is a young teenager. We have a rule in our house: "You don't have to talk to me, but you have to talk to someone we both know we can trust." Ms. Harriett is that someone for Jamie.

    We both must agree on the mentor because Jamie needs to know it is someone he can connect with and trust, and I need to know it is someone who shares the same values. This helps weed out some of the other voices that may not be helpful to Jamie. I want to avoid confusion in his mind about *right, wrong,* and *wise*. Jamie and I are similar in some ways, but unlike each other in other ways. I enjoyed sports, but he enjoys reading.

    We call Ms. Harriett Jamie's *adopted grand-god mother*. Jamie knows he can talk to Ms. Harriett about anything. They have a great relationship. Jamie expresses his love for people through acts of service. When Ms. Harriett needs something done like yard work, Jamie is quick to help her. As a bit of a trade-off, Ms. Harriett has taught Jamie how to cook and dance. She cuts up with him in a way I don't (or can't) and she genuinely treats Jamie like one of her grandchildren. (Jamie's adopted grandmother lives too far away for things like this to happen.) Jamie's school recently had a Grands Day (with a 1950s-themed "sock hop"). Guess who was honored to be invited? Ms. Harriett. They had a great time! We also go over to Ms. Harriett's for game nights or dinner. When we finalized Jamie's adoption, Ms. Harriett was there at the courthouse. It is like we have another family member! It helps that Ms. Harriett is a member of our church. In fact, most—if not all—of my sons' mentors came from within our churches.

VOICES

Not too long ago, Jamie made a very poor choice at school. It was a bad enough choice for Jamie to get suspended for a couple of days. Part of the consequences for Jamie was his confession to Ms. Harriett. You can imagine how reluctant Jamie was to tell Ms. Harriett. After some hesitation on the phone with Ms. Harriett, Jamie confessed his poor choice. Ms. Harriett reassured Jamie that she still loves Jamie, but she also let him know that she was disappointed. However, she had a very gracious way of letting Jamie know she was disappointed. A good mentor will love us no matter what, but a great mentor will also hold us accountable for our mistakes.

The reason we must be able to trust a mentor is that great mentors want the best for us and this means that sometimes, they must tell us things we don't want to hear. The other thing a great mentor will do is let me know if I am being too harsh as a dad. I know I can be a bit gruff when my kids make poor decisions. (This is one of the reasons I might not even be a 9 as a parent!) Mentors have a way of balancing out the reactions of parents. If I am too harsh with Jamie, he knows he can talk to Ms. Harriett, who will in turn hear my side of the story and correct me if I need it. (I also have mentors. There are some dads that I talk to so they can help me out when I feel lost or burned out.)

Mentors aren't perfect people. However, they create a *space* for another relationship where my sons can go to gain another perspective, get out of the house, and just have fun in a way they can't with me or their friends. Older people, like Ms. Harriett, want to know that they are making a difference with their lives. Younger people, like my son Jamie, want to know they are loved and accepted. (Every human being wants to be loved and accepted since a young age. When we don't feel loved or accepted, our ability to form our identity can become a real challenge because we feel very insecure.) Whether you are a parent or a mentor, nobody is perfect! In fact, young people also need to see how a believer makes a mistake but then also takes responsibility for the mistake, owns up to it, makes it right (if possible), and then learns to move on after having learned a lesson from the mistake. So, while Ms. Harriett is not perfect, she is perfect for Jamie and our family! I like to think that we are perfect for each other.

Here is the thing about mentoring: Like most things in life, we have made it much more difficult than it needs to be. We have *professionalized* youth ministry and made people think, "I can't do that." However, mentoring is more about getting to know each other and, once both people get to know each other, life-related questions are easier to talk about. Of course, during those conversations it is easy to share about faith questions and experiences. Life is the curriculum in mentoring.

In chapter 1 we examined the story of Elijah in 1 Kings 19. You may recall the story of Elijah and his showdown with the prophets of Baal on Mt. Carmel in 1 Kings 19. The basic story is that of idolatry and rebellion of Israel and King Ahab. Elijah had been trying to call Israel back to repentance to no avail. Then, the big showdown happens and Elijah is victorious. Right after the victory, however, Queen Jezebel threatens Elijah's life and Elijah runs. During this experience of fleeing, Elijah is exhausted, depressed, angry, despondent, and a litany of other negative emotions. Instead of chastising Elijah, God nourishes him with rest, food, and water. Even with God's intervention, Elijah twice insists he is alone. God reveals to Elijah that he has seven thousand in Israel who have not bowed to Baal. What pulls Elijah out of his depression? Hope for the future. This hope was found in the fact that Elijah began the process of mentoring Elisha to lead Israel into their next chapter of life.

The counter-intuitive realization was that Elijah was called to do something most of us would ignore when we are tired and exhausted. Elijah was now called to pour his life into Elisha. Instead of victory being found in a large battle, Elijah was restored by mentoring an individual. A word of caution here: I want us to remember that Elijah was first restored by God through rest, food, and an encounter with God. This is why we are called to seek God first through solitude, community, and then ministry. Unfortunately, many involved in ministry do this process backward. First, well-meaning people engage in ministry, then seek community, and then, when exhausted and burned out, we seek solitude and rest in Christ.

Questions

1. **Time:** Who is a trustworthy adult that you believe can be a "sounding board" for your child because they invest time in your child?
2. **Transparency:** Who do you think would make a good spiritual mentor for your child because you know they are authentic as a person?
3. **Trust:** Is there someone who would do all the right things when spending time with your child (he or she would meet with your child in public, has a long history of trust, and is a person of his/her word)?
4. Who would you be willing to share your time with, be transparent, and build trust?
5. What keeps you from spiritually mentoring someone younger than you? How will you overcome these chal-

lenges? Knowing most children and you will not have the social skills to ask for a mentor, who could you approach at your church that could benefit from you as their mentor?

Conversations With Your Children

- Ask your child, "Who is an adult, outside the family, that you enjoy hanging out with? Why?"
- Would you be interested in this person being a mentor for you? Why or why not?
- "Do you know that I love you?" "Do you know that I am proud of you?" (You may want to give some examples about their character that you are proud of.)
- After the reading and questions from the parent list and the mentor list, what are some other questions you would like to ask your child?

The Voice of the Church

The voice of the church is largely discounted by secular culture. Yet, for all the negative accusations that are being made against the church (some of them are well-deserved), we must remember that "the church" is much bigger than just the church in America. We need to consider this when we look at the diversity of the church (Christians as a group). The church has been engaged in feeding, housing, and clothing the homeless, the orphan, and the widows. The church was very involved in the civil rights movement. After all, Dr. Martin Luther King, Jr. was a minister who shared the teachings of Jesus. However, I am sure you know this too: the church is not perfect. (Do you see a running theme here?) Some churches can be downright mean to other people. I am just as sickened as anyone else when I hear about church leaders who have abused children, had affairs, stolen money, profited off of well-meaning people when trust is broken, and so on. There is no excuse for these things to happen. I cannot tell you how many times as a pastor and church leader I have been tempted to walk away from church. (If I feel this way, I know many others feel this way too!) The modern Western church has very much been influenced by culture rather than the other way around. Church attendance is on the decline—especially after Covid-19. Non-religious culture seems to be attacking the Church more than ever. (Around the world, the 21st Century saw more Christians killed for their faith than all the centuries before it.)[3] Fewer people are going into ministry to be youth pastors, children's pastors, lead pastors, or worship leaders. Some of this is because the culture has turned against, and will continue to turn against, religious people. (Some of this is deserved considering the wrongdoings of individuals in the church.) There are many pastors leaving ministry every day due to burnout. Some of this is because pastors are tired. They are tired of trying to do the right thing, seeing churches do the wrong thing and continually giving of themselves only to be underappreciated. Even good pastors leave the ministry because they become overwhelmed, feel less cared for, or feel less and less needed.

To tell you just how secular (non-religious) our society has gotten, in my experience as a youth ministry professor, I frequently have potential students and parents from Christian homes come by for campus visits. They will stop by my office

---

[3] https://aleteia.org/2017/06/30/are-there-more-martyrs-now-than-in-the-early-church.

and parents will often ask, "Can my son (or daughter) really make a living as a youth pastor?" Some parents have talked their children out of becoming a youth pastor or other ministry leader for fear of their children not being able to support him/herself. In my mind, these parents are asking the wrong question. In my mind, the question should be, "How do I help my child follow where God is moving and what God is doing in my child's life?" Life is more than a paycheck! When great young people become ministry leaders, the church's voice will be more respected. I tell my sons and my students, "Find out what you are passionate about. Once you find out what that is, you will find your purpose." Look for a vocation you are passionate about. You might even have to create a job or career that helps you live out your passion. For me, I was (and still am) passionate about God and young people. As I have gotten older, how I do youth ministry has changed, but my love for God, young people, and families has not changed. Experienced voices help the voice of the church.

The church around the world is very much more diverse than the church in America. We need to remember that God is not exclusively *an American God*. This correct perspective will help the voice of the church. In fact, religious nationalism is what caused the Pharisees and many others to miss Jesus as Messiah. (Even as an Army veteran, I like to say, "God bless the world," not just, "God bless America!") However, as imperfect as the church in America is, I have found some wonderful, deep, and meaningful relationships that have helped me make it through life and parenting. Trust me, if there is anyone that has been burned by church leaders, it is me. However, my relationship with God's people and with God Himself is bigger than the imperfect churches in which I have attended and served. As imperfect as it is, most of the time the church is a voice worth listening to. Just like my parents are imperfect, just like my mentors are imperfect, and just like I am imperfect, the church is imperfect as well! (Any human organization is imperfect. Every person can find fault with any organization.) It is also true that some voices are wiser than others, even in the church.

While many people (including "Christians") are talking badly about the church, we must remember that the church holds a special place in God's heart. In fact, the Bible teaches that the Church is "the Bride of Christ" (Ephesians 5:21–33; Revelation 19:7–8). That sounds strange to many, but it is symbolic language. If I had a close buddy named, Joe, and I said, "Joe, I love you my friend, but I cannot stand your bride!" How long do you think Joe and I would remain friends? You can't attack a man's wife and think he'll be okay with it! The voice of the church is unique because the church is the bride of Christ.

Can the church change? Absolutely. The church must change! However, can you name any perfect group of people or organization? You will never find a perfect church and, if you ever did, the minute you entered it, it would become imperfect. Even with its imperfections, the voice of the church is vitally important to a young person.

Just like Ms. Harriett has become family to us, the churches I have attended have become like family—and you don't give up on family. What would it be like if, after my sons came to live with me in my house, they started acting up and I just gave up on them and kicked them out? I truly would be a horrible person. Why is it then that we so easily give up on the church? If you don't like a church as an organization, first start trying to see the individuals in the church. See if you can connect with them in a way that will make you grow wiser. The voice of the church isn't just its good work or even its doctrine. If the church is the people, then their voices become the voice of the church.

Being very involved in a local Bible-believing church can give your children wonderful experiences. Through the church, I have been able to travel the world on mission trips and minister to people who are far worse off than I am. I had the privilege of serving them (but in truth, their humility and grace changed my life more than I changed theirs.). I have taken youth and families on trips that have enhanced their lives and given them a deeper worldview. I have gone to camps, played games, enjoyed friendships around bonfires and meals, learned together, grown together, cried together, laughed together, celebrated together, encouraged each other, prayed for each other, got onto each other, and loved each other well. Of all the organizations in the world, the church can be the best one to be involved in. The voice of the church can change someone's life forever.

Christ is very inclusive. In fact, Jesus came to die for the entire world. Jesus said the free gift of salvation is for every single person who will receive it. The fact that all are welcome to join makes the church a very unique group and gives it a special voice in the world.

As I have said, my sons and I have gained a family by being involved in different churches. I have brothers and sisters all around the world. Europe, Africa, Asia... you name the place and there are brothers and sisters in Christ all over the globe. There are not many groups or organizations that offer such a large and diverse membership. This makes the voice of the church better. It does not matter their skin color, nationality, gender, or anything else. If someone trusts in Jesus, they are my brother or sister.

Local churches and denominations are not always correct. Teaching our children to leave a toxic church is a valuable lesson. Why would I leave a church and take my family elsewhere? Here are a few examples: abusive leadership, a congregation of hateful people, a church that doesn't stand for truth as found in the Bible, tradition, reason, and experience. These are good reasons to recognize harmful voices and leave. After you leave, it is important to find another church. I have heard people say, "I can believe in God and not have to go to church." Well, they are sort of right, but the problem with this thinking is they are only hearing their own voice on who God is and what it is like to follow Him. They begin to shape God in their own image, beliefs, likes, and dislikes. They do not have people to challenge them to think differently, and that is unhealthy.

Why is the voice of the church still important? Frankly, the church should be able to push us in ways that both encourage and inconvenience us. This is clearly stated in Hebrews 10:24–25, "And let us consider how we may spur one another on toward love and good deeds, not giving up meeting together, as some are in the habit of doing, but encouraging one another—and all the more as you see the Day approaching." To "spur one another on" means to stir up or to provoke. This is a strong word that indicates sometimes we must be pushed onward toward good works by others. This is exactly what younger people are doing today. Many of them are leaving the church because the church seems to be irrelevant to real-life and not caring about the world. When the church preaches *the cultural mandate to exercise dominion over the earth—to be fruitful and multiply* people will see we care about more things than buildings, crowds, and money. The voice of the church repeats the cultural mandate that God gave Adam and Noah (Genesis 1:26–28; 2:15; 9:1), we show that we care about the things that matter to God!

So, how can the church help gain a voice in the lives of young people?

1. **Learn how to listen to your young people by equipping them for ministry.** We must stop saying, "Young people are the future of the church," but do nothing to train and equip them for leadership. It is as if churches think young people will magically want to be involved in church leadership when they become adults. (Even when they become young adults, it seems churches do not trust them with important positions and places of trust.) If we do not help young people have a voice and take ownership of ministry as they grow up, by the time they are in 10th grade, they will have already checked out of the church to pursue places where they think they can make a difference. Churches must move from *observatory* ministry, where everything is done for young people, to *participatory* ministries that help young people discover and express their spiritual gifts and calling. The typical time young people *get to serve* is on the obligatory, once-a-year youth Sunday, the nursery, or VBS. These approaches are only participating in further systemic abandonment because churches are using young people to fill their agendas rather than helping young people discover their own unique ways to contribute to the life of a church. Just about any volunteer position that can be filled by an adult can serve as a training ground for youth! When children and youth are raised to know that they matter in a church, they are more likely to stay connected to the church.

2. **Become more missional minded outside the walls of the church.** This may be hard for many church leaders and parents to hear, but unless the church in America becomes more mission-oriented and gospel-cause driven beyond the occasional short-term mission trip, our young people will find a way to fulfill their passion to help (minister) in other places away from the church! Developmentally, young people want to know they matter, they can contribute and make a difference, and their voices matter! They can, and will, find their identity in people and organizations that are willing to see a bigger picture of gospel ministry outside the walls of the church, or they will find purpose somewhere else that is not the church. In fact, just about every community has some sort of ministry to help those in need. Church partnerships are great ways to have more regular mission experiences. I will push even further and say, to be truly missional, maybe churches should consider getting involved with secular organizations such as your community's programs to help families, protect children, and provide foster care. These organizations are often overwhelmed and would welcome the support of local churches. You should encourage your youth to be involved in para-church organizations such as Fellowship of Christian Athletes, Young Life, or similar organizations. If you fear "losing your kids" to some other organization, that should force you to ask questions about what they are doing right and what your church may not be doing right. We are better together.

3. **Be more mindful of non-traditional families.** Family dynamics are changing. An increasing number of families are now non-traditional or permeable. However,

the church in America seems to still be geared toward traditional families. Whatever the non-traditional family might look like, we still have a responsibility to "visit the Samaritan woman" and offer the gospel. In fact, in this occurrence, you will note that Jesus went to the Samaritan woman, not the other way around (John 4:1–42). Jesus met her where she was and through that encounter, many became believers! Where has that missional mindset gone?

4. **Help adults become stronger disciples.** I cannot begin to tell you the number of adults who want to disciple their children but do not know how. I often ask adults, "How have you been discipled?" Their response is either through church worship attendance or something like Sunday School or a small group. This might have helped them gain some biblical knowledge, but knowledge without practice and intentional mentoring does not seem to produce disciples. In fact, the Pharisees were full of knowledge but failed to know how to practice the things God intended. They also were full of pride and arrogance and put themselves above others. I fear we are seeing much of this today. Church leaders must find congregation members who are hungry for growth and then help those members put their faith into action. Discipleship, like a missional focus, must go outside the walls of a church into everyday life. Teaching and practicing spiritual disciplines are a great start! (I recommend texts such as Richard Foster's *Celebration of Discipline* and Dallas Willard's *The Spirit of the Disciplines: Understanding How God Changes Lives*. The complaint I often hear is, "Well, I don't like to read," or "These books are too difficult to read," or some sim-

ilar thought. In other words, we allow Christian adults to use immature responses to get out of spiritual formation and discipleship. When these excuses surface, it is no wonder that Christian parents do not know how to disciple their children. We must stop making excuses! If a person does not like to read we can provide audio books and great video series. If we want to develop life-long disciples of our children, we need to do deeper discipleship of our adults and parents!

5. **Keep current on youth ministry research.** The rate of cultural change is increasing exponentially and is primarily driven by technology. The "generation gap" of understanding is now between 5–7 years. What worked ten years ago does not work today. Life for teenagers has become much more complex (hence the whole premise of this book). Many church leaders and parents want to go back to *the youth ministry they once had* without recognizing the challenges that face youth and youth workers today. I encourage all church leadership to read Mark DeVries' book, *Sustainable Youth Ministry*, especially if there is a lot of turnover in youth ministry leadership. Mark DeVries' book is written with keen insight as to why youth ministries fail and how leadership can change that equation. To stay on top of the rapidly changing culture of youth, I recommend frequently visiting Dr. Walt Mueller's Center for Parent/Youth Understanding website, www.cpyu.org. Dr. Mueller is a recognized expert on youth culture. I also recommend *A Biblical Theology of Youth Ministry: Teenagers in The Life of The Church* by Michael McGarry.

6. **Provide intentional intergenerational ministry with a ministry advisory team.** Many young people also

leave the church due to a lack of intergenerational ministry, rites of passage, and feeling valued in the church. Frankly, even most *family-based* youth ministries are geared toward nuclear families that have a *traditional youth ministry model*. Spending large sums of money to have a youth ministry does not equal discipleship success. The goal of discipleship is to raise up lifelong committed disciples of Jesus who reproduce other Christians. Even though I have literally worked with tens of thousands of young people throughout my career, I am not sure that more than a couple of hundred are lifelong committed disciples of Christ who produce more Christians. (I wish I had known back then what I know now!)

The truth of the matter is this: Young people need an increasing number of wiser, more mature Christians to speak into their lives and our wiser, more mature congregation members need the vitality, innovation, enthusiasm, and excitement that young people bring into the life of the church! There are a significant number of churches that are lamenting the lack of young people involved in their worship service or church, and yet most churches are not willing to get out of their *comfort zone* to make young people feel welcome. In fact, we must go beyond making young people feel welcomed to giving young people supervised ownership of the life of the church! To do this, young people need wise mentors.

I will use an analogy of music to explain bringing the young and the old together. (How many churches have suffered the *worship music wars*?) The truth is the church needs both hymns (the older) and modern worship music (the younger), with an understanding that both should be theologically sound. Hymns have stood the test of time and often speak to the cerebral truths of God. Modern worship music speaks to the heart and can be very moving. Worship should speak to the head (hymns), the heart (contemporary worship), and the soul (truth). When I teach my students, they understand that adults, who are cognitively developed, appreciate intellect (the head) while adolescents often learn through emotive means (the heart). Not to belabor the point, but we should appeal to the head, the heart, and the soul. Remember Jesus' words, "Love the Lord your God with all your heart and with all your soul and with all your mind" (Matthew 22:37).

The church still has an important voice in the lives of young people and young people should be encouraged, trained, and equipped to offer their voice to the church. Intergenerational ministries that consider both traditional and non-traditional family ministry opportunities will be a must for the future church! Churches will need to offer both in-person and virtual connectivity. A social media presence may be the very first thing a potential guest may see before he or she steps into your church. Think about how digitally savvy young people can be and use that to your benefit. Churches that want to grow and are serious about discipleship will need to stop placating laziness and excuses. Church leadership must continually challenge their assumptions and constantly educate themselves and their leadership on the fast-paced changing culture around them. Everyone needs to be willing to learn from others. Missional, non-competitive (and even secular) partnerships will be essential to churches who want to remain faithful to the call of sharing the gospel with lost people.

Discipleship needs to be understood for what it is—a call to take up the cross and be willing to die to ourselves so others might live (Luke 9:23). Church leadership will need to become less hierarchical and more empowering. Church leadership will also need to stop insisting on the right to be right, rather insist on taking up their own cross and serve as Jesus did (Matthew 20:28). Finally, the church must move beyond ministry of the 1980s, whether that is youth ministry or outdated approaches and embrace that God is constantly doing new things. As the prophet Isaiah stated, "See, I am doing a new thing! Now it springs up; do you not perceive it? I am making a way in the wilderness and streams in the wasteland" (Isaiah 43:19).

Finally, I want to add something as a word of encouragement to smaller churches. Larger churches have a knack for doing outstanding programs, but sometimes (not always) the programs become more important than the people. Smaller churches have a knack for being more personal and people-oriented rather than program-oriented. Yes, Jesus ministered to the multitude (the program, if you will) but He also deeply discipled twelve. There are resources out there to help smaller churches. I mentioned D6 Family Ministries as a great resource: www.d6family.com. I also recommend Youth Ministry Consultants: www.youthministryconsultants.org. Most churches in America are smaller churches with less than 100 in Sunday morning worship services. They also have youth in their churches but often lack the resources to have extravagant youth ministries. Most church youth workers are volunteers and feel under-trained and under-resourced. Youth Ministry Consultants (YMC) will provide low-cost or no-cost coaching for youth workers. This is possible because donors give to YMC to make this happen. With today's digital options, it is also possible to connect seasoned youth workers and coaches that will help coach and mentor smaller church youth ministries.

Questions

1. **Time:** How much time have you invested in your church? Are you willing to stick it out even during tough times? How much time does your church invest back into you and your family?
2. **Transparency:** Are you honest with your church leadership by offering solutions you are willing to implement, rather than just complaints? Is your church transparent in its leadership?
3. **Trust:** Are you honest about your spiritual growth and roles you play in being responsible for that growth? Can people trust you as a disciple of Christ? Is your church leadership as trustworthy (or more) as you are?
4. Have you been *burned* by a church before? If so, how did that impact your perspective of churches? How did it impact your walk with Christ?
5. How can you gain wisdom from negative church experiences and use that wisdom to help guide others?
6. What are you doing to make your church better at discipleship? What are you doing for your family to help them grow closer to Christ through being with other believers?

Conversations With Your Children

- Who are some adults that you connect with at church?
- What do you like about our church? What do you dislike about our church? What would you change about our church if you could?
- How does our church help you become more like Jesus?
- What are some ways you would like to serve in the church?
- Who do you see at church who reminds you of Jesus? How can we be more like Jesus at church?
- After the reading and questions, list any other questions would you want your child to answer.

The Voice of Diversity

Tribalism is full of practices that seek to silence the voices of those who are different from their own tribe. It saddens me that the United States of America is still struggling with issues of diversity—especially when it comes to truly listening to voices that are different from our own. This being stated, some things need to wait to be discussed until an appropriate age is reached. Diversity has become an all-encompassing word sometimes used to shame others who hold a different moral perspective. In agreement with Dr. David Elkind, *some* discussions are not appropriate with children, such as sexual identity issues. This is a complex issue and, for this reason alone, it is a discussion that should wait until a child's cognitive ability is on par with the conversation.[4] Unfortunately, this discussion is increasingly becoming forced to be had at ever-increasing younger ages. This is simply unacceptable. It is easy to see the conflict between the world's perspective on sexuality and the Christian—and biblically defined—perspectives on sexuality. Our allegiance is to the Kingdom of Christ, not the mandates of man. In fact, this is the very reason early-century Christians were martyred—their allegiance was to Christ, not Rome.

For the sake of simplicity, this is not the type of diversity I am writing about. I have been fortunate to have traveled to and through approximately 45 different countries around the world. I love the richness and diversity I experience when traveling. When someone travels, the smart folks learn to appreciate the differences in culture, vibrant foods, clothing, languages and accents, artwork, people, and customs of the places they visit. When traveling, it is wise to appreciate a different culture rather than critique it. I learn so much more from other perspectives. That is the joy of traveling—getting to know other people and cultures that are different. I get a sense of wonder at God's incredibly diverse creation.

As diverse as America is supposed to be, we do not often listen to the voices of *the other*. (The other is someone different from us.) This has caused a lot of issues in our country. America has become increasingly separated and polarized by religion, politics, race, gender, ethnicity, and social issues. Instead of finding appreciation for *the other*, we seem to want to gather people around us who have the same voice and

---

[4] A recent, and very helpful book to consider, is *When Children Come Out: A Guide for Christian Parents* by Mark Yarhouse and Olya Zaporozhets. Certainly age-appropriate conversations need to happen in certain life stages and the aforementioned book is excellent for parents who find themselves questioning the sexuality of their teens.

perspective as our own. Once again, this does not mean that we must acquiesce to every perspective—especially when it comes to morality and integrity.

There is a similar mentality and limitation between the statements, "I don't have to go to church to believe in God," and "I am only going to hang out with people who think like me." When we close ourselves off from others, we miss out on the diversity in life that God offers us. In fact, teenage years almost seem to thrive on being like everyone else because teens want to be accepted. If we think, act, dress, and speak too much differently than our peers, we may fear being rejected and not fitting in. How many of us, deep down, want to be the popular person? Even adults sometimes want to be accepted to the point of not sharing our minority opinion. Of course, there are some who enjoy being recognized as the *unique one* in the family, but also want to fit in with their our own cliques, peer groups, tribes, whatever you want to call it.

Think about this though—God is the creator of diversity! How many species of fish, birds, animals, planets, stars—and so many other things—are out there for us to appreciate? This does not even take into account diversity in the spiritual realm with different types of angelic beings! It has been said that the most segregated institution in the United States is the church. And the most segregation time each week is Sunday morning.

What is it about being together with people who are different from us that we resist? Children go to one part of the building, youth to another, adults to another, and older adults to another. It is with great infrequency that we come together. It can seem like too much diversity is like a lot of noisy voices, but is it? In fact, it is just the opposite. Here is what I mean: if you want to gain some diverse perspectives, you must sit with someone different from you and hear their story. You don't have to agree with every point they make, but active listening is a way that you earn the right to be heard as well.

Though I have a multi-denominational background that typically runs in the Protestant circles, I received the gift of a deeper Trinitarian theology from a Greek Orthodox priest during one of my seminary experiences. I am forever grateful for this particular experience. I was taking a course on spiritual formation and the professor had arranged for his predominantly Protestant students to attend worship at a Greek Orthodox church. It was fascinating to see all the rich and beautiful tapestries of worship that combined seeing icons, incense, prayer, and music—all done in significantly different ways than I had experienced. The best part came after the worship experience when my fellow seminary students were able to have an open dialogue with the Orthodox priest in which we had a great time of questions and answers. We had a great discussion about the role and person of the Holy Spirit. I developed a more robust Trinitarian theology because I was able to engage in a small group discussion with someone different from me but who was also theologically grounded. Ultimately, the Bible is our authority but understanding of deeper theological topics comes through conversations that are much more personal rather than dogmatic. This is also why personal conversations and deeper Bible study with small groups can be so effective in faith formation.

Have you ever tried to have a personal conversation with someone in a very noisy environment? If you really want to get to know someone, you usually find a quieter environment to talk. It is difficult to have meaningful conversations in the middle of a large, noisy crowd. When we get to know others who are different from us, our worldview becomes just a little bit larger. Even if you are not in an ethnically diverse community, you can certainly meet people different from you. Maybe you should get to know someone who is your grandparent's age. If you are in an ethnically diverse area, take the opportunity to get to know someone different from you in a meaningful way.

I have learned so much more about life by being with, and listening to, people who are different from me. Even while writing this, I took a break to run to the local grocery store. I live in a smaller community but even here I experienced two God-sent moments to validate the very purpose of this chapter. Waiting in line at the Starbucks in the grocery store, I had an incredibly encouraging conversation with a woman in her 80s who was part of the German Baptist community in our area. Women in this group wear long, plain dresses and bonnets similar to the Amish. As we talked, we discovered that we had way more in common when it comes to our Christian faith even though our lifestyles were obviously different.

As I was leaving to get gas, a gentleman from India saw my Toccoa Falls College faculty sticker on my truck window and asked what I did. I must admit, I did not know where this conversation would go, but I told him I am the Associate Professor of Youth Ministry at Toccoa Falls College. You could see the excitement in his eyes as I simultaneously asked him what he did for a living. He stated that he worked in IT. He not only was a Christian, but had recently been talking with his wife about starting a Bible study for the youth in their church. Isn't it wonderful to see God answering his prayer by meeting me, a youth ministry professor. They were a diverse voice to me and I was a diverse voice to them.

Intentionally seeking opportunities where there is a great variety of diversity, will help you will learn how valuable a diverse voice can be in your life. Toccoa Falls College has a large contingency of Hmong students. The Hmong people are wonderful, gracious, and warm people![5] I had the privilege of leading a workshop at a large Hmong gathering. I was one of maybe three Caucasian people among the hundreds of Hmong people. I was made to feel so welcome that I did not feel like a minority. You see, in the Body of Christ, there are no minorities! We are all one in Christ! Galatians 3:26–29 says it all. In fact, in Christ, our outward ethnic expression has no bearing because we are "clothed in Christ" (Galatians 3:27b). This is what it means to have diversity in Christ. It is our inner self, being formed by Christ so others can see Christ on the outside!

Helping your teen discover God's voice through diversity also helps them to discover the love of God for all humanity. This love in and through diversity is not only found in Galatians 3, but it is also mirrored in 1 John 4:19–21: "We love because he first loved us. Whoever claims to love God yet hates a brother or sister is a liar. For whoever does not love their brother and sister, whom they have seen, cannot love God, whom they have not seen. And he has given us this command: Anyone who loves God must also love their brother and sister." This is also why Jesus adds a clause in His Great Commandment. That clause is, "and the second [commandment] is like it…." You see, there is equality in loving God and loving each other exactly with the same diligence and passion. The entirety of the Great Commandment reads as such: "Jesus replied: "'Love the Lord your God with all your heart and

---

[5] For more information on the Hmong people, visit www.hmongamericancenter.org.

with all your soul and with all your mind.' This is the first and greatest commandment. And the *second is like it*: 'Love your neighbor as yourself'" (Matthew 22:37–39, italics added for emphasis).

All of this comes together to give a voice to missions, evangelism, discipleship, and spiritual formation. I have taken students on several local, national, and international mission trips. Often, it is the students who receive a blessing and joy from serving those who are different from them. Mission trips are often life-changing experiences. I have also taken just my sons to feed the homeless in Atlanta, Georgia. I encourage the students and my sons not only to provide help, but also to listen to the people's stories. This is another way we expose our young people to other diverse voices. Some of those voices are healthier than others, but even this is a learning experience as it helps our young people discern between wise and unwise voices.

One final thought on engaging in diversity and hearing different voices. As a college professor, I also challenge my ministry leadership students to hear other voices by attending Bible-believing churches that are unlike the ones they grew up in. I am not asking them to leave their denomination or throw aside their doctrine. However, I am asking them to hear the gospel and Scripture from other perspectives. My goal as a Christian educator, professor, and parent is to teach young people to learn *how* to think biblically, not *what* to think. Often, my students come back sharing how they gained a new perspective through experiencing a worship service or Bible study through different lenses. Isn't this our role as people who want to nurture faith? Don't we want our young to see and experience God for the fullness that He is through the diverse people He created?

Questions

1. **Time:** What amount of time have you spent listening to diverse (but biblically sound) voices?
2. **Transparent:** Are you aware of, and in touch with, your own personal biases or prejudices against different people or denominations? If so, what are you doing to overcome them?
3. **Trust:** What are your "markers" for knowing if you can trust a voice that is different from what you have always heard?
4. What do you or your church do to help young people hear and engage with biblically-sound, diverse voices? If there is no engagement, what kind of plan can you develop with your children to make this happen?
5. What is the most diverse or different group you spend time with engaging in spiritual conversations?
6. If you had to take an honest look, what are some biases or fears you may have in engaging with other denominations or people of faith? If it is not bias or fear, what keeps you from engaging with people different from you and your family?

Conversations With Your Children

- How do you sometimes hear other messages that are different from what our family believes or values? How do you handle those conflicting messages? (You may have to give examples.)
- When is it good to hang out with and listen to people that are different from us? When is it unwise to hang

out with or listen to people that are different from us? (Focus more on values and worldviews, not cultural differences.)
- Who is someone in your life that is different from you that you really get along with? What makes that relationship work?
- Who is someone in your life that is different from you and that you don't get along with? What causes the relationship to be difficult?
- How can we be a witness for Jesus to people who are different from us?
- After the reading and questions, list any other questions you want your child to answer.

The Voice of God

In a 2018 article published online by *USA Today*, columnist Maureen Groppe delved into the spiritual and political fray on the topic of hearing from God. Vice President Mike Pence caught flack for stating that he hears from Jesus. Joy Behar, one of the co-hosts of the television show *The View*, insinuated that Mike Pence and his faith displayed signs of mental illness. Behar also claimed to be a Christian who, apparently, has never heard Jesus (God) talk to her. What Behar may seem to forget is that communication is not simply limited to audible or verbal dialogue. There are many forms of communication that are *unspoken*. Body language, facial expressions, cultural imagery, icons, and so many other forms of communication exist. If you have been with a person, a spouse, a child, or even a teammate, for any extended period of time, you can know what they are communicating without using words.

No doubt, Behar would also disagree with many biblical precepts and teachings and yet, for Christians, the Bible is one of the primary ways God uses to communicate with humanity. Many people claim to be Christian, but aren't true followers of Christ. James 2:19 says, "You believe that there is one God. Good! Even the demons believe that—and shudder." The reason demons shudder is because they do not obey God's Word and they know they will be paying a price for it eventually. Even Jesus said, "Not everyone who says to me, 'Lord, Lord,' will enter the kingdom of heaven, but only the one who does the will of my Father who is in heaven" (Matthew 7:21). Do you see it? Only those who do the will of the Father. This means not just listening to Scripture, but doing what it says (James 1:22). I could spend chapters writing about the legitimacy and inerrancy of God's Word, but that would take way too much time and there are other more scholarly people who have undertaken that assignment. I have read other *holy texts* from many other religions, studied philosophical approaches to life and yet, the Bible is the only text that truly makes consistent sense throughout the entirety of the text. Not only are there very simple and conscious truths in Scripture, but the deeper you dig into the contexts of the writing, the more truth you find existentially and subconsciously. Nominal Christians cannot embrace the truths of Scripture or the fact that God can speak to His followers. I do not mean to find fault, but not believing Scripture or not hearing from God are a couple of ways to find out who has more of a secular mindset and who is pursuing their spiritual development.

There is a huge difference between exegeting Scripture and eisegeting Scripture.[6] To exegete simply means to contextually

---

[6] The prefix *ex* typically means *out of*, while *eis* means *into*.

interpret Scripture. In other words, the Scripture speaks for itself based on knowing the context of the author, who it was written to, word studies, what time period the text was written, what cultural elements of that time need to be considered, what truths it spoke to the people of that day, and digging into every possible background aspect of the text. It is only after these steps are taken that a proper contemporary interpretation can be given of that Scripture text. Eisegeting Scripture is the opposite. Eisegesis is putting a modern narrative or construct over Scripture that either misinterprets, or ignores the original meaning of the Scripture to appease modern sensitivities or to lay one's own interpretation upon the Scripture. We see this a lot today—especially when it comes to sexual issues that have been around since the beginning of humanity.

Listening to the voice of God is a lot like listening to authorities or experts in our lives. Sometimes we like what the experts have to say, sometimes we don't like what the experts have to say because it is an inconvenient truth to what we want to do with our own lives. Whether parents, teachers, scientists, or whomever the authority may be, humanity has a proclivity to dismiss the voices they do not like to hear—even if it is a voice of wisdom. Case in point: How many young people went through an education process like the D.A.R.E. (Drug Awareness and Resistance Education) program? And yet, with all that information and scientifically proven results of smoking and doing drugs, young people still choose to smoke or do other drugs. You see, having information is not enough. Information and data, without knowing how to properly apply that knowledge, lacks wisdom. It is not always a question of "right or wrong," rather, what is the wise thing to do? What decisions are the wisest based on the information and positive outcomes? This is called having a "fruitful life" mentioned in

VOICES

Genesis 1:28 and John 10:10. Proverbs 14:12 says, "There is a way that appears to be right, but in the end it leads to death." Proverbs 16:20 says, "Whoever gives heed to instruction prospers, and blessed is the one who trusts in the Lord."[3]

This is how we hear from God:

1. **God speaks through His Word.** Scripture is God's love letter and historical account of His interactions with humanity. It shows His holiness (perfection) and how we could never live up to that perfection to live with Him in Paradise. (If there is any imperfection in Heaven, it cannot be Heaven.) This is the Old Testament. The Gospels basically become the story of how God made all things right for all humanity by Jesus Christ taking on the payment for sin through His death on the cross. The rest of the New Testament (except for Revelation) is early Church history and letters from the apostles instructing believers how to follow Jesus Christ. The final book of Revelation shows how God will complete everything. (This is, of course, a very rudimentary explanation of the Bible.) People who do not understand the intricacies of the Scripture will of course disparage it. Secular people, who have no academic or theological training, have been trying to disparage Scripture for hundreds of generations.

2. **God speaks through other people.** God speaks through other believers. We are called to encourage one another (2 Corinthians 13:11; 1 Thessalonians 4:18; 1 Thessalonians 5:11; Hebrews 3:13). This is the point of gathering for worship, Bible study, fellowship, and prayer as previously discussed. It is the point of having godly mentors. Proverbs 15:22 says, "Plans fail for lack of counsel,

but with many advisers they succeed." In fact, God used Moses as His mouthpiece to speak to the Egyptians and the Hebrew people (Exodus 4:15). Why would we take counsel from worldly or secular individuals who doubt the validity of Scripture and a living God who desires to speak to us? What secularists cannot fathom is the necessity of healthy two-way communication between God and His children for a relationship to even be possible. One false theology that has been perpetrated by well-meaning people is, "We are all God's children." (There are lots of false pop-culture theologies out there like this, such as "All sins are equal,"[7] etc.) Saying we are all God's children is a nice platitude meant to bring comfort to folks, but this teaching is contrary to Scripture (John 1:12, Romans 8:9, 1 John 3:10), which clearly communicates who the children of God are. You cannot be a child of God if you do not accept His authority through the written and living Word of God.

I should also mention something that many would not like to hear: God can speak even through our enemies. God often used the enemies of the Hebrew people to discipline them due to their rebellious ways. As I mentioned in the discussion on diversity, we need to be willing to at least listen to our enemies because if we do not listen to our enemies, how can we ever be expected to love them (Matthew 5:43–48)?

3. **God speaks through circumstances.** Psalm 119:105 states, "Your word is a lamp for my feet, a light on my path." First, notice the lamp is for the feet. In other

---

[7] All sin is an afront to a holy God, but Scripture demonstrates some sins are more damaging and have greater consequences.

words, the Word does not cast a long-distance light rather it illuminates the path step by step. This means that we are to trust God in the circumstances of life. I suspect that if God showed us everything there is to our future, we would do our best to try to change it. (We already do this when we choose not to listen to His Word so we can do our own thing.) Trusting God in all circumstances is the essence of faith—we hope for what we do not yet see. This is the most perplexing thing about prolonged anxiety in the life of a Christian. Yes, Christians can experience *some* anxiety, but prolonged, sustained, and intense anxiety shows a lack of trust in God. Too many Christians have put their hopes into the temporary circumstances of life. Listen to the words of Job in Job 13:13–15:

> Keep silent and let me speak;
> > then let come to me what may.
> Why do I put myself in jeopardy
> > and take my life in my hands?
> Though he slay me, yet will I hope in him;
> > I will surely defend my ways to his face.

I am certain Job experienced anxiety that came along with his very real physical, emotional, and spiritual torment, but notice that Job still has his hope and trust in God. Very few of us will experience what Job went through, yet we seem to experience increasing anxiety for far less suffering. Trust in God as He speaks through circumstances, but do not listen to the circumstances alone.

4. **God speaks through solitude.** This is a bit redundant but requires a point all its own. Simply put, busyness keeps us from taking time in solitude to hear from God. We can also fear what we might hear from the depths of our hearts and souls. The heart and soul engaging in a prayerful life are what Theresa of Avila termed, the "interior castles" of our lives (Sanchez, C. 2015).

The primary way God speaks to us is through His Word. I have spent most of my life not just studying the Bible, but literally trying to find the faults in it. The more I have tried to tear it apart (through logic, philosophy, science, and social sciences), I have found it stands up incredibly well. The more I dig into it, the more truths I find. I like to consider myself a smart man. I have an undergraduate degree, two master's degrees, and a doctorate. Even though I am a professor in a ministry leadership department at a college, not all my degrees are religious. (I had to promise Jamie I would not pursue another doctoral degree until he is out of the house.) As a life-long learner, I have learned to investigate, synthesize, and reject information. I've learned to make arguments and, most importantly, learned how to think based on research. My point is this: as an educated person, I am not smarter than the Bible. There is so much truth in the Bible that *its voice* has shaped me. It has shaped me in how I view people, how I love them, how I forgive them, how I know that no situation or person is beyond redemption or love and so much more.

The Bible is full of wisdom like no other book. I have read the Quran, the Ghita (Hindu scriptures), and many other texts. None of them stand up to the Bible. Even secular philosophies come up short. Along with mentors and the church, the Bible is a voice that helps me become a better person. The person I was 5 years ago is not the same person I am today and much of this I owe to *the voice of the Bible*. This is THE most important book for Christians and churches.

Of course, Scripture helps us to hear the voice of God since it is the written Word of God. Not to sound too repetitive, but the fact is that we often hear the voice of God through our parents, a mentor, our church, and diverse experiences as a way of teaching us how to listen to the voice of God. This helps us to understand that if any of these people or organizations were dysfunctional or unhealthy, we often have a dysfunctional or unhealthy understanding of God and His voice. The reason this is true is that God uses these "quiet voices" to teach us how to listen for His voice. Remember the occurrence of Elijah? He heard the voice of God, not in the earthquake, the wind, or the fire. Elijah heard the voice of God in a whisper. However, certainly, Elijah had heard from God through His spoken word, His commandments (Scripture), cultural contexts and circumstances, and even the circumstances that were both victorious (victory over the prophets of Baal) and difficult (the death threats uttered by Jezebel).

When we learn to listen to other healthy voices like our parents, mentors, church, and diverse perspectives, they become little whispers that point us toward God. How many of you, when you are about to decide something, you "hear" the voice of your parent in the back of your brain whispering, "I wouldn't do that if I were you!" Maybe you hear this voice more often, "You need to clean your room!" (Even by reading this, and your parent isn't standing in front of you, you can "hear" their voice in the back of your brain!)

In a way, this is how we hear God's voice—through times of solitude and silence. Richard Foster writes, "Our fear of being alone drives us to crowds and noise" (Foster, 1998, p. 120). Remember, the most noise comes from the shallow end of the pool! To hear from God, we must silence all the noise by seeking solitude in order to listen to the tranquil, whispering voice of God. Jesus often did this. It should be noted that there is a significant difference between being alone (solitude) and lonely (a lack of community). The more we read God's Word (the Bible), the more we listen to the voice of the church, the more we listen to godly mentors, and our youth pastors and the more we hear from other believers from other Christian backgrounds, the more we actually can hear God whisper into our hearts and our minds. It is as if we have trained our souls to know when God is speaking to us.

Remember, even Jesus went to the mountains to pray—especially because of the busyness and hustle of the ministry demands (Matthew 14:23). Despite what many may think—prayer is simply talking to God—it is a two-way dialogue. God speaks to us in that *still small voice* that has been shaped by Scripture, godly parents, mentors, and leaders. We cannot hear that still small voice in the shallow end of the pool where all the noise is. It is no wonder those who think they are Christians, but do not believe God can speak to them, are too busy listening to the voices of the world rather than being able to hear the voice of God. The "inner voice" of God, that same whisper that Elijah heard, is drowned out by their own voice as well as the voices and noises of the secular society.

Even a multitude of ministry leaders (and parents) get a certain formula wrong when it comes to engaging in ministry or engaging in our family life. We often do ministry (caring for others and our families) then, when things get hard, we seek community and then when we are overwhelmed, we seek solitude. This formula is backward. First, we need to rest and seek solitude. For the Jewish people, the Sabbath is the beginning of a new week, not the end! Once we are rested, we should seek community to help us navigate the upcoming week of ministry. It is after when we have rested and sought community that we should then actually engage in the work of ministry!

It is your primary responsibility to nurture your relationship with God, by spending time with Him and hearing His voice, which allows you to then help your children hear His voice as well. If your children cannot hear His voice through yours, it may be that you are not listening to the many ways God is speaking to you. When God does speak to you, you should point this out to your children so they know how you know when God is speaking! Wouldn't it be a great day when disciples do not have to ask the question, "How do I know when God is speaking to me?"

Questions

1. **Time:** How much time (honestly) do you use to cultivate your relationship with God?
2. **Transparency:** How real and honest are you with God? Do you try to hide shortcomings or sin from Him?
3. **Trust:** Where do you have a difficult time trusting God (for instance, finances, life decisions, family, career, etc.)?
4. Can you pinpoint times when God has spoken to you through:
    a. His Word
    b. People (Friendly or Enemy)
    c. Circumstances

5. How often do you take time to listen to God's voice in solitude?
6. What scares you about being alone?
7. Have you found yourself overwhelmed with the busyness of day-to-day living, so much to the point that you do not hear from God? What steps will you take to change this?
8. As a parent, ministry leader, or mentor, why is it important to model—and speak about—hearing from God?

Conversations With Your Children

- If you had to describe God, what would God look like to you?
- If you had to describe the character of God, what would God's character be like?
- Who most reminds you of God?
- How do you hear God speak to you?
- How do we know the Bible is God's Word? If we know that the Bible is God's Word, how does reading and knowing what is in the Bible shape our lives?

Chapter 3
Small, Loud Voices

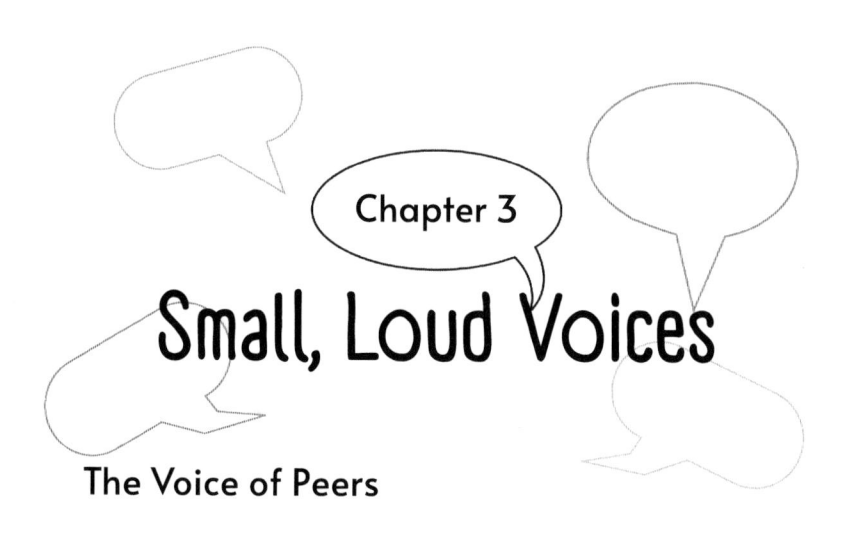

The Voice of Peers

While writing this book, I was unsure about the placement of peers. Should this section go under big, quiet voices or small, loud voices? The truth is, they could go under either. It depends on what type of friends your child is surrounded. If their friends encourage your child to listen to wise voices and make wise decisions, then they can go under the big, quiet voices. However, if they are peers that encourage your child to listen to unwise input and make unwise choices, well, they fit into the small, loud voices category. The reality is that parents may wish they could choose good influences among their child's peers, but in reality, this is impossible. Most kids spend 8 hours per day in a school environment hanging out with hundreds (if not thousands) of their peers. Add on top of that, social media where the average amount of digital interaction is approximately 11 hours per day, it is quite impossible to monitor, let alone choose your child's friends. Parents do have a say in who their child predominantly hangs out with by saying who is invited into the parent's home, whose home their child goes to or spends the night, which families their child can travel with, etc. Let's go back to the three "Ts" to see if we can look at helping our children make wiser decisions regarding their peers.

Time: In the parent voice section, the question was asked about how much intentional time do you spend with your child? I should have mentioned there about starting with some *devoted time expectations* for your family. It is easier to start these habits when your children are younger. For instance, we have certain devoted time that very few things get in the way of. Here is an example from our family of a typical week: We attend church on every Sunday and most Wednesdays, have family dinner every night (with no electronics at the table), and look forward to our *family night* with pizza and games on Saturdays. We aren't perfect, but we are very consistent. This builds into your children a sense of family time and shows them that you *want* to spend time with them. As your children get older, more activities that will begin to compete with your family time, but you have set a pattern and a habit that, believe it or not, your kids may reinstitute when they become parents. As your child gets older, they will drift away from you to spend more time with peers—it is a fact of life. You can still *negotiate* a once or twice a month family game night. Remember, you are the parent! As your children *drift away*, here are some questions you need to ask: Do you know who your child spends most of their social time with (in school or out of school)? Do you know who your child spends time communicating with digitally?

Transparency: Has your child been open with you about his or her friends? Time and transparency are a bit easier to monitor before your child starts driving, but what happens when your child gains more independence away from you when driving, taking a job, or any of the other things older high schoolers do? For me, I have made it clear that having a cell phone is a privilege for my children because I pay the bill. Having a car is a privilege because I typically bought the car and pay for insurance. Think about it: the average teen could not afford their own phone or car insurance. Also, the average teen does not NEED to have a car or a phone. Will this force you to be creative? Absolutely, but most teens work to buy gas, food, and maybe their own clothing. Unless they are truly contributing to the household finances, phones and cars are a social convenience. As a parent, you provide for the needs but can control the social conveniences. Phones have made it convenient for us to stay in touch with our children because most homes have working parents, but convenience should not be the driver of what keeps our kids safe in their short-term decisions that can impact their long-term mental and physical health. My children understand that if they are hanging out with the wrong people and making poor choices, I shut their phones down and take the battery out of their vehicle.

Why am I making all these obvious statements? I am making these statements because time and transparency build trust! We have an app on each of our phones that gives real-time information such as their location, speed of vehicles, crash detection, and more. This gives me peace of mind and allows me to quickly provide emergency help. Transparency is the foundation for trust. As a parent, you should be transparent about your expectations and your children need to learn to be transparent with you.

Trust: If your child begins hiding things from you, that is a sure sign that poor decisions are being made. These poor decisions can create arguments and break trust. We must remember that maturity is also influenced by nature as well as nurture. The pre-frontal cortex of the brain is responsible for logical decision making but it does not fully mature until around 24 years of age. After your child does something extremely reckless and you ask, "Why did you do that?" how many times have they answered, "I don't know!" When this happens, they aren't being deceptive. Rather they are driven by a lot of emotions that override the logical part of their brain. That emotion might be fear, a desire to be accepted, lust, or any other hormonally driven response. While this is normal, it also serves as an opportunity to help them exercise their pre-frontal cortex and walk through how to make logical decisions. No matter the circumstances, consequences must be in place before and during poor decisions.

I want to share another little story about friends and poor choices that happened to me. Remember, all my children were adopted and this has some bearing on the story. I received a call from one of my sons around 3:00, while I was at work, asking if he could go downtown to walk around with his friends. We live in a small town and Main Street is no more than a half mile or so long. I agreed and reminded him to be back home around 5:00 for dinner. When I came home around 4:30 from a shorter day of work, my son was already home. That struck me as odd because most teens will take every moment they can to be with their friends. I didn't think much of it other than I stated, "You are home kind of early." He responded that he had a headache and he was not feeling well. I acknowledged and started making dinner. When it came to dinner time, my son stated that he was not hungry either and that he was going to lie down. I checked to see if he had a fever, had drank enough water, and all the other questions a parent might ask to see if their child is coming down with something. Everything appeared normal.

I had to leave soon for an evening church leadership meeting. As we were wrapping up the meeting, I received a phone call around 8:00 from my son's school principal. She was checking to see if my son was okay. I was confused.

I asked, "Well, what do you mean?"

She stated, "[Your son] was in a really bad car accident today."

I was baffled. "Can you tell me more?"

She said that my son was with a group of friends and the young lady driving lost control of the vehicle, rolled down an embankment and, if it were not for a tree, the vehicle would have rolled into the river. While most of the students are okay, a couple of them are in the hospital.

As you can imagine, I was freaking out! "Thank you for your call and letting me know. I need to go handle this right now!"

As I was mentally putting the pieces together, my military background and years of first-aid training helped me realized that my son had a concussion! People who have had a bad concussion should not sleep unmonitored—the consequences can be bad.

I woke my son up and said, "Hey, you need to come with me because I need to take you to the hospital." I *very briefly* told him how I knew what had happened and my priority was to make sure he was safe and healthy. I did tell him that we would have a conversation about the situation later. I don't want to go into the rest of the details only because they are not valid to this point. When we eventually had the discussion about his initial untruthfulness he admitted that he was afraid and didn't want to disappoint me. He knew he had made a bad decision. My response to him was, "Son, I love you no matter what, but here is something important to remember: I would rather be disappointed by a poor decision you made than have my soul crushed if you had died!" I reiterated to him that if he ever found himself in a bad spot due to a poor decision with his friends, he should call me and I would come to get him—no questions asked. This does not mean we would not have a discussion later.

A couple of years later, when we were talking about something else, my son told me that was the point he knew I loved him. This is a very difficult realization for many older adopted children to have. My two older sons have had a much more challenging time in the area of choosing good friends. As they have gotten older, they would readily admit to this. During their adolescent years, I have had to give the consequences I have mentioned and then some. My role, as someone who has a matured pre-frontal cortex, is to sometimes make decisions my immature children do not agree with or like. However, I must be the mature adult until they become one themselves.

As a reminder of this verse, 1 Corinthians 15:33 says, *"Do not be misled: 'Bad company corrupts good character.'"* I have seen this truth lived out in so many ways through the years. I want to share an example from one of my college students who wrote the following. She had given her life to Christ at age 12 at a revival, but then writes this about her experience later that year: *"Now, I wish I could say that I chose Jesus every day from that point on, but I did not. Later that year, after accepting Jesus,* **I started hanging out with the wrong crowd in middle school.** *This was the first time I was introduced to alcohol and unhealthy relationships."* (Name redacted, Spiritual Formation Class, Fall 2022, Toccoa Falls College.)

Years ago, I mentored a young man named Will (real name protected). Our relationship grew through our time together as we studied the Bible, had conversations, shared meals, and just hung out. He went on youth trips with us and I just saw a lot of great character traits in Will. He was so good at baseball that he got a college scholarship at my alma mater. I could tell that Will was pulling away from our time together, church, friends, and more. Whenever I tried to talk to Will about whatever was going on, he did not engage in the conversation. I was very perplexed (and honestly, a little hurt). Come to find out, Will started made poor choices in friends at college. These unwise voices encouraged drug use. At first, it was just a little marijuana and then it led to harder things like meth. In a matter of a year, Will went from a person of great character with a college scholarship for baseball to a drug addict who dropped out of school. This experience was crushing to my soul.

I have seen too many young people who traded the wise voices in their lives for unwise voices. Ultimately, many of them paid a very steep price. For some students, it was more important for them to be accepted by a different group of peers than it was to be accepted by those who genuinely cared for them.

Many parents do not realize the importance of trusted relationships at home starts as a young child. When children and youth feel like they have secure attachments to their parents or caregivers in the home, they are more inclined to forge bonds of trust that will help navigate them through a confusing culture and help them to more easily determine the positive voices in their lives. Once again, I recommend reading works by Erik Erickson. I have included a link in the reference section that not only gives an overview of Erikson's work, but also helps explain the stages of childhood psychosocial development (McLoed, 2018).

VOICES

An important goal in parenting is to help the home become a sanctuary for children to return when voices get confusing. The combination of time, transparency, and trust between parent and child will hopefully create this atmosphere of love. When your child begins to love his or her peers, it leads to new issues in their lives. But the good news is that it is never too late to work hard at building a more positive and influential relationship with your child.

Questions

1. Do you know who your child's closest friends are? Do you know who your child's *online friends* are?
2. How do you help your child understand that friendships are not always worth compromising? (In other words, there are worse things than being lonely if their friends lead them down the wrong path.)
3. How do you help your child navigate bullying or other negative relationships?
4. How does your love for your child give them the strength to choose wise friends?

Conversations With Your Children

- Who do you enjoy spending the most time with?
- Are your friends honest with you?
- Who are your closest friends? Who are your *online friends*?
- How can you tell who will be a good friend and who will be a not-so-good friend?
- Do you ever have to deal with bullying?

The Voice of Consumerism

I remember growing up watching cartoons on Saturday morning. While watching them, commercials would come on pitching everything a kid could want—everything from sugary cereals to toys. Each product was designed to be appealing to children. Whether it was a cartoon character selling cereal to some really cool looking peers playing with a certain toy, the intent was to appeal to my seven-year-old heart and mind. Even as a kid, I so desperately wanted a certain toy that I practically begged my parents for it. I did extra chores to earn money or placed it on my birthday or Christmas list. My parents did not have a whole lot of money so, when I got the toy, I was ecstatic—until I found out the toy did not work like it did in the commercial. I remember seeing those huge foam airplanes that kids would throw in the commercials. The plane seemed to glide on forever and do incredible loops and tricks. When I got my plane, however, I discovered on my first toss that the wings would come off making the body of the plane plunge to the ground. The next time I threw the plane, I tried to toss it ever so gently thinking that would fix the problem only to get the same results. After five attempts to make the plane fly even a few feet, I gave up. What a waste of money and emotional energy!

Do you remember being a kid and wanting that special something? You would beg, hope, dream, and save up for it only to be disappointed? One other product I remember from when I was a kid was an action figure called, Stretch Armstrong. Looking back at the advertising for this iconic toy, I'm reminded there is very little you can do with the toy. Here is what the box states in the marketing: "Stretch him, pull him, tie him in knots. When you release him, he uses his super strength to slowly return to his normal shape!" I discovered after having the toy for about an hour, there is only so much you can do with Stretch Armstrong until you get bored! It became another dust-gathering toy!

Remember the movie, *A Christmas Story,* and the main character, Ralphie? What a great nostalgic movie, full of childhood wonder, rites of passage, and truths! Do you remember exactly what Ralphie so desperately wanted for Christmas? It was an "official Red Ryder, carbine action, 200-shot, range model air rifle, with a compass in the stock and this thing that tells time." We have all had these desires, but one of the funniest themes running through the movie about marketing had to do with the "Little Orphan Annie Show" that Ralphie would listen to on the radio. He could not wait to get the "Little Orphan Annie" decoder ring. Ralphie had to send in a huge number of Ovaltine labels in order to receive his secret decoder ring to decipher secret messages, thereby allowing him to be a member of Annie's Secret Society. After all those labels and impatiently waiting on the decoder ring to arrive in the mail, the message Ralphie decoded was, "Be sure to drink your Ovaltine!" Ralphie realized he had been duped. "A crummy commercial," Ralphie exclaimed right before using some foul language to show his contempt. Do you ever feel like you have been duped—even as an adult—when it comes to being disappointed by marketing? Many of us have purchased products that do not live up to the hype.

One of the courses I teach at Toccoa Falls College is Youth Culture. While these documentaries are becoming a bit outdated, I have my class watch two PBS documentaries. They are called, *Merchants of Cool* (2001) and *Generation Like* (2014). Several things happen as my students engage in these documentaries. First, they are repulsed by the films as they see how media (even before the digital age) has objectified, used, and sexualized young people. Second, their eyes are opened to just how much they have been manipulated by corporate America. With *Merchants of Cool* being just over twenty-years old and *Generation Like* being almost ten years old, students can see a progression of how savvy and sickening marketing has become. In today's culture, exposés such as *The Social Dilemma* (2020) are beginning to show how easily social media manipulates truth, lies, and human nature. The voice of consumerism is strong.

If you wonder why it feels like it is so difficult to keep up with the influences your teenagers are under, it is because it *is* difficult, if not impossible. The generation gap (understanding between generations) used to be about 20 years between generations. Now, the generation gap is 4 to 7 years. Much of this is driven by technology and the growing disconnect between young people and adults. In fact, it is such a challenge that there is an ever-increasing degree of ephebiphobia in our culture. Ephebiphobia is "a fear of young people." Ever since corporations and companies found out that parents spend a lot of "disposable income" on their children and teens, they have become *missionaries* who want to profit from what they know about young people. Many see corporate America becoming increasingly malevolent missionaries who study your kids, culture, social media, and social influence to get to know and influence them better than you can. This is even more so since as corporate America not only goes after *your* disposable income, but they are also like blood-thirsty hounds who go after your kids' money as well! They do not care about the moral or social development of your child. They only care about profits. This sounds a bit harsh, but if you do not believe me, watch the three documentaries I mentioned and tell me if I need to retract these statements.

While America has flourished under capitalism, increasing corporate greed has led to the justification of immorality at many levels. Whether it is sexualizing young people to sell a product or CEOs receiving outrageous bonuses after running companies into the ground, it does not take long to see that consumerism can be, and the love of money is, the root of all kinds of evil. First Timothy 6:10 spells this out clearly: "For the love of money is a root of all kinds of evil. Some people, eager for money, have wandered from the faith and pierced themselves with many griefs."

Unfortunately, when it comes to consumerism and flashy things, the church has found itself resorting to similar approaches as secular marketing when it comes to attempting to attract individuals to participate in the programs. Something has gone awry when our priority is to attract people to our church rather than attracting them to Jesus! If we were a missionally-driven people, we would understand that most evangelism, by definition and necessity, would happen outside the walls of a church. Deeper discipleship should happen *in the church* and incorporating efforts that bring others to Jesus. Then, when a person comes to Christ, we can encourage them to become a part of the family of Christ where His body meets. I believe the church in the West became so *seeker-friendly* that we have become weak in discipleship. In fact, it is this very reason so many denominations have abandoned orthodox beliefs in order to appeal to those to whom the gospel might be offensive. In other words, even in church we have become consumer friendly! This has led to what German Theologian and modern martyr Dietrich Bonhoeffer would call, "cheap grace" (Bonhoeffer, 1937). This form of *discipleship* costs a person nothing in the way of sacrifice but ultimately can cost them their soul. How many people have we left at the altar of cheap grace requiring nothing of them except to be *saved*?

It was the offensive teaching of Christ as living bread that caused many to turn away from Jesus. We must remember that many people turned their backs on Jesus because of hard teaching. We see this in John 6:60–66:

> **On hearing it, many of his disciples said, "This is a hard teaching. Who can accept it?" Aware that his disciples were grumbling about this, Jesus said to them, "Does this offend you? Then what if you see the Son of Man ascend to where he was before! The Spirit gives life; the flesh counts for nothing. The words I have spoken to you—they are full of the Spirit and life. Yet there are some of you who do not believe." For Jesus had known from the beginning which of them did not believe and who would betray him. He went on to say, "This is why I told you that no one can come to me unless the Father has enabled them." From this time many of his disciples turned back and no longer followed him.**

Try that for a marketing strategy! Start your marketing campaign by telling people to follow you to their deaths (Matthew 10:38; 16:24; Mark 8:34; Luke 9:23), put others first (Matthew 19:30; 20:8; 20:16; Mark 9:35; 10:31; Luke 13:30, Philippians 2:3–5) love your enemies (Matthew 5:43–44; Luke 6:27, 35) and so many other messages that are the exact opposite of the worldview of corporate America. Corporate America wants you to be the life of the party, win at all costs, and annihilate your opposition.

Don't get me wrong, there are benefits to capitalism. A competitive market leads to innovation, better products, deters monopolies from occurring, and keeps prices in check. Competitive industries create jobs. However, unchecked capitalism can lead to greed, power, influence, and lack of morality that has become a corrupt form of capitalism. Not all capitalism is evil. Remember, it is the *love of money* that is the root of all evil (1 Timothy 6:10). Yet, many have become wealthy, benefitted from capitalism, and have given back great sums of money to various charities. Capitalism, when practiced ethically and morally, drives competition that improves products and, sometimes, people's lives. However, when corporations sway government officials through lobbying and campaign contributions (or their close cousins known as bribery and extortion) to win votes that are only in the interest of the corporations, that is corruption. We can easily see how these approaches are the opposite of Jesus' teachings. Jesus even stated, "Truly I tell you, it is hard for someone who is rich to enter the kingdom of heaven" (Matthew 19:23).

Have you ever noticed that the more money or the more stuff you have, the more human nature tends to want more? A great question to ask is, "How much is enough?" Consumerism is not just about how much we make, how much we spend, or how much we save when it comes to money. The very root word of consumerism is *consume*! As I have gotten older, I realize the more stuff I accrue, I do not own that stuff—that stuff owns me! If I own a house where my family and I live, there are maintenance costs involved with owning that home. Add on a car, a camper, or a boat. These things also require maintenance. Now, add on a second or vacation home, a second car, etc. All require time and maintenance. This is time and money I could reserve for more important things like building meaningful memories with my family. Regardless, I am no longer consuming things, those things are now consuming me! This way of thinking also bleeds into our entertainment and digital media consumption. If left unchecked, entertainment and digital media begin to consume our time, our affections and even our money. As an adult, how often do you find yourself scrolling through social media, or playing a video game, for a temporary escape from your monotony only to find that more time has passed than you intended? Consuming social media can consume us and this is especially true for our children.

This is also another point where both "nature and nurture" come into play. By nature, we are in many ways, consumers. We must have food, clothing, shelter, clean water, and clean air. What human beings need (nature) is quite minimal compared to what human beings *want*. What has been *nurtured* in us in our consumer-driven society is the desire to have more. Media, advertising, and consumption can nurture unhealthy perspectives within us. Media is a sort of social contagion. Think about when you were growing up and some product was marketed right at you. Do you remember thinking, "Oh, I *really* want that!" For some of us, the thought may have even been, "I *need* that!" This is especially tempting for young people because they are trying to fit in. Remember, the primary task of adolescence is identity formation. Entangled in this reality is that young people are trying to find their identity through their peers and activities. If they are playing basketball with their peers and many of their peers are buying a certain pair of shoes that have been heavily marketed, guess what your child is going to want? Marketers make it sound like your child must have a certain pair of shoes to make their basketball game more effective. Marketers often blur the lines between want and need—and this is done with intentionality. The voice of consumerism is intentionally deceptive.

Let's be honest about something: Sure, there may be several products that might make our lives easier or improve them, but very few products are truly life changing. Most products are presented as a need when they are actually a want. Theologically, salvation is a need—and it is life-changing. Of all the things we need and want to give our children, a life-long committed relationship with Jesus Christ *must* make everything else pale in comparison. Jesus addressed this when he stated in Mark 8:34–36: "Then he called the crowd to him along with his disciples and said: 'Whoever wants to be my disciple must deny themselves and take up their cross and follow me. For whoever wants to save their life will lose it, but whoever loses their life for me and for the gospel will save it. What good is it for someone to gain the whole world, yet forfeit their soul?'"

It is not enough to simply come to an altar, make some sort of decision to trust Jesus but then live the rest of our life unchanged. Yes, we are justified by the work of Christ on the cross, through His resurrection, and with His ascension. However, if we recall, one of the initial calls of Jesus to His disciples was to take up their cross and follow Him (Luke 9:23). Make no mistake, this was a call to die. The cross was the device used for the execution of prisoners. The cross was not a piece of jewelry as we know it today. To wear a cross is akin to wearing a piece of jewelry fashioned like an electric chair! Wearing a cross does not make one a Christian. A consumer Christian mentality hijacks the meaning of the cross. Just as we must learn the difference between wants and needs in our spending habits, we must learn the difference between wants and needs in our spiritual life.

Discipleship is costly, but when it is done right, it is well worth it. Jesus gave us two short parables about the value of walking with Jesus.

The kingdom of heaven is like treasure hidden in a field. When a man found it, he hid it again, and then in his joy went and sold all he had and bought that field. Again, the kingdom of heaven is like a merchant looking for fine pearls. When he found one of great value, he went away and sold everything he had and bought it (Matthew 13:44–46).

Christianity is not something to be consumed, yet it is something that should consume us. Are we helping our children develop an insatiable appetite for walking with Jesus in a costly manner or are we using religion as a tool to keep them in line? Is going to church just an add-on, like an accessory to an outfit? Shouldn't the church be a natural extension of who we are? Do we go to fellowship to worship God, connect with brothers and sisters in order to be encouraged, and then see the church as a launching place for our ministry to the world? Have we made church and our spiritual growth nothing more than a Stretch Armstrong—something we were enamored with but realize it has lost its luster because it was something we consumed? Despite what secular culture or Christendom proclaims, we still need the church and the church still needs us. We cannot disciple our children on our own nor can the church. We need each other. I pray our faith is not something that we consume, rather our genuine day-to-day walk with Jesus becomes a consuming fire that not only consumes us, but also ignites a consuming fire in our children and those around us (Deuteronomy 4:24; Hebrews 12:29).

So, let's use our three filters once more to help us determine what type of voice consumerism plays in the lives of our children.

Time: Compared to all the other things that consume our time, how much time do we spend intentionally discipling our children? I will say more about this in the section on social media, but the amount of time we spend in digital engagement far outweighs the time we typically spend in meaningful pursuits. Think how much time you and your children are exposed to marketing. We see things on billboards, television programs, radio, and many other sources. We are even more exposed to marketing through our phones and social media. Algorithms now have pinpoint accuracy to tempt us to purchase *stuff* due to the things we search for on our smartphones. We are constantly bombarded with ads more than we may have an awareness of. Here is the thing though—marketers do not care about your time and they certainly do not care about taking time away from your family and other important things. How much time do we spend maintaining our stuff?

The saying, "time is money" is so very true, but in our case, our time wasted has taken away value on things that matter. As we can easily see, consumerism does very little to give back time. Certainly, some things can give back time. Dishwashers have become incredibly convenient and just about every home has one, but think about the conversations you can have when washing and drying dishes together. This is a bit of a hyperbolic example, but it makes a point. Every time we buy the next thing, whether that is another car, an RV, a motorcycle, or some other toy, how much time do we have to work to pay it off? How much stress does it create when things get tough financially? These are important things to think about because working harder for the toys actually creates more stress in our families.

Transparency: Let's face it, very few marketing pitches are 100% transparent. No marketer is going to tell kids, "You're going to get bored with your Stretch Armstrong after 30 minutes of playing with it." I have heard many boat owners say that the best two days of their life as a boat owner were when they purchased their boat and when they sold it. They realize the amount of time and effort it takes in maintaining these things, but it would not be a good marketing tool for boat manufacturers to tell potential boat owners about their best two days! In fact, most producers and marketers try to appeal to how much fun you will have with your family, but they do not tell you about the additional expenses and stress these things will bring into your life because these things now own you.

Trust: Like our Ovaltine example, do you really trust marketers? While products do help make our lives better, are they worthy of our trust? Certainly, there are some brand names we trust more than others, but things never really solve relationship issues. In fact, there have been many breakups and divorces over wasted money and time. To make my point clearer, how many of us have heard of families who have become estranged over stuff that is given to them when a loved one dies? Everything will eventually wear out, but relationships are designed to be eternal. We can never put our trust in stuff and yet, how much time do we spend pursuing stuff rather than relationships?

Questions

1. How much of your time gets consumed by *stuff* compared to pursuing Christ? What message does this send to your children?
2. Compare your fiscal decisions when it comes to purchasing stuff you need, stuff you want, and money you give to the Lord's work and charity. For most of us, a very small percentage of our finances is given to church or other charities. What does your fiscal modeling say to your children about needs, wants, and generosity?
3. How have you seen your children (or you) influenced by marketing? Do you have discussions with your children about the influence of marketing and consumerism?
4. How do you help your children know the differences between the voices of needs, wants, desires, and generosity?

Conversations With Your Children

- Have a conversation with your children about something they really wanted. Was that item satisfying? If so, for how long and why was it satisfying? If not, what was disappointing about it?
- Create a challenge to see how many types of ads we are bombarded with each day by counting them every time we are aware of an ad. Were there any memorable ads? What made them memorable? Which ads worked best and why?

- Have a conversation about how we are shaped by our needs, wants, and generosity.
- Ask how your family can move away from consuming to giving. How can you do this in your spiritual life?

The Voice of (Social) Media

As I mentioned in the introduction, not everything is inherently evil or inherently good. How humanity uses innovative tools is what makes the tools either evil or good. Media and social media are good examples of this. Though closely related, media and social media also have significant differences. With media, it is the content developers and producers who publish a narrative. With social media, it is often individuals who put out a narrative. With the advent of *liquid post-modernity* and the insistence that there are no absolute truths, it is no wonder most individuals have a difficult time discerning truth from lies. Polish sociologist Zygmunt Bauman theorized that in the Modern era (prior to 1960s) societies believed that life was filled with expected ways of functioning. Deviations from those expectations were irritating and temporary changes to the norms of a society. They also believed that a perfect world could be achieved through rational and comprehendible norms. This way of thinking was considered "solid modernity." In solid modernity, there were—at least in theory—accepted social metanarratives for societies. These metanarratives were stories of a society that were considered true and commonly shared. In liquid post-modernity however, social structures, relationships, values, and even communication have become increasingly fluid. What has become more valued is not a shared common story accepted as truth, rather the micro or individual story is seen as truth. You may have heard it this way, "That may be your truth, but it is not my truth."

This is true when it comes to media or social media. Without absolute truths, everything and anything can be manipulated. As a professor, I regularly read scholarly research. It is shocking how often I identify statistics that have been manipulated. Technology is a significant contributor to innovation, but there are also significant ethical and moral questions that need to be asked.

In fact, there is even new Artificial Intelligence (AI) that can create original content without a human author. As if plagiarism wasn't a concern for those of us in the academic world, now we must be concerned about whether or not a student actually wrote an article, a poem, or any other creative written work. It is getting more and more difficult to tell the difference between reality and fiction. We see this blurring between reality and fiction happening in an increasingly polarized world. It is easy to find so-called experts presenting "facts" on issues from polar opposite perspectives.

While common sense would argue that 2 + 2 = 4, the door has been opened to refute even scientific truths. No matter where you are in your perspective of Covid-19, its subsequent strains, or whether you are for or against vaccines, the lack of a belief in truth has led to an ever-increasing polarization of the world. Coupled with a lack of truth, distortions of information for personal or organizational gain, and a lack of moral bearing, societies that are going in these directions are bound to experience chaos. History repeats itself.

Using the filters of time, transparency, and trust, social media ranks way down on the scale of reliability! Not only is it necessary to have a conversation with our children about the good and bad of media and social media, but we must also give them an understanding of how culture is changed through inaccuracies, manipulation, and lies. Polarization emerges when there are competing narratives. Western, American, rugged individualism has been the perfect incubator for liquid post-modernity. Liquid post-modernity not only argues against absolute truths in regard to history, morality, religion, etc., but it also seeks to establish a new metanarrative by insisting the individual (micro) narrative is the most important metanarrative. The irony is that all the competing narratives (whether individual or group) create a metanarrative of competition, confusion, and anger—hence the polarization in the West over everything from government, religion, and even science. We have created a world where nothing and no one is to be trusted. In Western, liquid post-modernity, the prevailing metanarrative is the micronarrative. In other words, individual or group truths and stories are more important than societal truths or narratives. Historically, every way of human thinking can implode upon itself. Liquid post-modernity makes an absolute truth claim that there is no absolute truth.

Historically, and in a very simplistic overview, ancient cultures ascribed truth to a deity or deities. In the 1300s, the Dark Ages ended and the Renaissance was born. It flourished through art, expression, creativity, and philosophy. The Enlightenment begins around the late 1600s but finds its beginnings in Descartes' proclamation, "*Cogito, ergo sum.*" While there may have been misinterpretations of Descartes' epiphany, "I think, therefore I am," there is no doubt this philosophy shaped the way of Western individualism. What kept the rugged individualism in check were powerful institutions and their desire to preserve societal norms. Individualism and creativity allowed for free thinking and ushered in the scientific revolution. Science replaced deities and even *the self* as the authority over life. As the modern age progressed and the horrors of World War I and World War II, faith in science as the answer for truth wanes to the point where the individual experience and identity become the authorities for life. We are now in what became known as *liquid post-modernity*. Zygmunt Bauman introduced the concept in response to modernity and the holocaust (Best, 2014). Along with how we have already defined liquid post-modernity, one of the main theses of this philosophy is that science has failed because it developed more ways to wipe out mass humanity than it has developed to help it.

Enter the marriage of the digital age with liquid post-modernity. For a new philosophy, or metanarrative, to prevail, it must attack, undermine, and destroy the former prevailing metanarrative. In Western cultures, we can see this in the form of the increasing influence and prevailing metanarrative of secularism. This newer metanarrative must attack the roots of Christendom or supposed *Christian nations*.[8] Regardless, a secular narrative must attack Christendom to prevail. While Christians proclaim God as the Author of Truth, liquid post-modernity and secular humanism have come together to establish the individual as the authors and arbitrators of truth. However, we must remember that philosophies, over time, change and yet God's Word remains.

---

[8] It could be argued that America and other Western nations were not really Christian nations, rather they were more likely Christendom nations—a collusion between church and state. Since the Edict of Milan in A.D. 313 by Emperor Constantine, Christianity went from a persecuted religion to the accepted religion of Western nation states. This laid the foundation for centuries of Christendom, but we must understand that Christendom is not Christianity. Jesus even stated that His Kingdom was not of this world (John 18:36), but we have seemed to have forgotten this fact.

First Peter 1:22-25 says,

> Now that you have purified yourselves by obeying the truth so that you have sincere love for each other, love one another deeply, from the heart. For you have been born again, not of perishable seed, but of imperishable, through the living and enduring word of God. For, "All people are like grass, and all their glory is like the flowers of the field; the grass withers and the flowers fall, but the word of the Lord endures forever." And this is the word that was preached to you.

Many secularists reject Christianity due to the many mistakes Christians have made. Certainly, organized religion under the banner of Christianity, but what was actually *Christendom*,[9] has made very gross mistakes and atrocities. However, I suspect another real reason for secular humanists to reject Christianity is the truth claim of Jesus Christ as the authority as "the way, the truth, and the life" and no one coming to the Father except through Him (John 14:6). To admit the authority and lordship of Jesus Christ means a necessary rejection of the self as the authority over one's own life. Human truths often conflict with Kingdom truths and a human being must decide who he or she wants to be the ultimate authority in his or her life.

For those of us born before the year 2000, we are digital immigrants. Those who are born after 2000 are digital natives.

---

[9] *Christendom* refers to the territorial or state religion, especially during the Middle Ages, that attempted to make Christianity a form of government instead of a personal relationship with Christ.

Liquid post-modernity, with its assertion that there is no absolute truth, self-creates cultures inundated with individual micronarratives, lacks objective truth, and creates a lack of trust in governments, media, corporations, science, history, and so much more. It is no wonder there is increased anxiety among our young. Now the media outlets and social media platforms can create competing narratives that create division, anger, and hatred simply because we cannot trust anyone or anything. Welcome to cultural chaos and confusion! Think about how much of this chaos and confusion our digital natives are engaged in with approximately 11 hours per day being involved in digital media, FOMO (fear of missing out), and the lack of moral boundaries created liquid post-modernity.

I call this *fluid post-modernity* because everything in Western culture has become fluid. Truth, politics, economics, jobs, gender, sexuality, species, taboos—everything is fluid and changing. This is what happens when the individual is more important than truth and digital natives are exposed to countless numbers of individual truths and perspectives. This is why parents must be involved in monitoring digital content and consumption while discussing difficult topics with their children. As believers, we can offer our children an antidote to the chaos and confusion created by digital, liquid post-modernity: truth.

To move away from the academic for just a moment, media and social media, with their potential for sensationalism, distortion of truth, and the pursuit of *15 minutes of fame* has allowed our young people to create their own narratives. Since 2019, research has shown that the top desired career for young people is to be a social media influencer. Whether making videos for gaming, fashion, philanthropy, or other pursuits, young people see becoming a social media influencer as their top goal to make a living. If you watch the video I recommended earlier, *Merchants of Cool*, it will be easy to see the negative places those choices can take a young person. For so many young people, rather than "making it," they face the harsh realities of rejection or find themselves compromising moral and ethical values.

Take the case of Steven Fernandez. Once a popular skater who found fame by shooting skate videos in his early years, Fernandez eventually found himself creating media stunts that moved away from skateboarding into inappropriate sexualized behaviors to stay on top of his social influencer game. These stunts eventually landed Fernandez in legal trouble being accused of rape. I am sure his influencer name, "Baby Scumbag" did not help perception. What we have seen is the development of a generation that values the possibility of being a social media influencer at almost any cost. When it comes to a teens desire for popularity so they can become monetized through social media, there are very few, if any, adults offering wise counsel to protect these teens from poor decisions (Conti, 2017). We need to consider the significant pull of identity, influence, and making money that come together and result in potentially horrendous consequences. If making poor decisions can generate an identity as an "influencer" and pay the bills, some teens, and even their parents might willing push the limits of socially acceptable behaviors or morality. We can use our three filters to rate the value of the voice of media and social media in our lives.

Time: Though our children and youth spend a great deal of time in the digital world, not all of it is edifying, encouraging, or equipping. Think of the countless hours spent on social media, engaging in so many ways of thinking that could be contrary to truth. Now add the countless hours of video games.

VOICES

Comparatively speaking, how much time does your child use in authentic educational pursuits? As for media in general, we must teach our children that too much focus on the world can cause increased anxiety and depression. Significant amounts of academically, peer-reviewed research have shown that too much digital media consumption leads to mental health issues including anxiety, depression, and anger—especially when it comes to cyberbullying and hostile messaging.[10] I have experienced this as a pastor, a professor, and a parent. I must constantly remind myself to fix my eyes on Jesus, the pioneer and perfecter of my faith (Hebrews 12:2). We must remind our children of this fact as well. If we as parents and our children would spend just a tenth of the time they invest in digital interaction with the Bible, we would all become much more biblically literate!

Transparency: We must teach ourselves and our children to remember that most of what is on the internet cannot be trusted simply for the lack of transparency! Though secular society rejects absolute truth, there is truth to be found. Truth brings stability and consistency. Stability and consistency are necessary for a healthy child and adolescent development. We can all name news networks that have their own slant on the truth—especially in the political world. This happens in both the progressive and conservative worldviews. We must teach

---

[10] For some helpful books, I recommend *Behind Their Screens: What Teens Are Facing (And Adults Are Missing)* by Emily Weinstein and Carrie James. While not a "Christian" text, this book has a lot of good information about the digital world and teens. I also recommend *Every Parent's Guide to Navigating Our Digital World* by Kara Powell, Art Bamford, and Brad M. Griffin, which does incorporate a Christian worldview with practical applications for parents and teens. This book is mentioned on page 90. Another helpful book is *Screen Kids: 5 Relational Skills Every Child Needs in a Tech-Driven World* by Gary Chapman and Arlene Pellicane.

our children to seek out truth and not be easily susceptible to ideological perspectives. Both media and social media must be approached extremely cautiously when it comes to truth. While there may be the denial of "social contagion," even the CDC (Centers for Disease Control) and other mental health care professionals recognize the impact of media and suicidal ideation (Ortiz, et. al., 2018) and eating disorders linked to social contagion (Forman-Hoffman, et. al., 2008). Are we truly supposed to believe that sexual identity, sexual activities, and perspectives are not formed through social contagion and excessive media exposure?

Trust: Through the presentation on time and transparency alone, it should be enough to show that the positive influence of media and social media is tenuous at best. Given the other perspectives of systemic abandonment, lack of accountability on the Internet, increased messaging of secularization, and a rejection of common morality in Western culture, there is enough evidence to show that media and social media should be viewed as suspect. Trust can only be gained through truth and transparency.

A final word: we should not wholesale reject media or social media. We must simply know how to engage in deeper research and use Scripture, tradition, reason, and experience as theological and worldview filters. This approach to engaging in practical theology is known as the Wesleyan quadrilateral. We must then also approach information by thoroughly engaging in academic research. As for ways to think about the digital interactions between our children and ourselves, I recommend, *Every Parent's Guide to Navigating Our Digital World* by Powell, Bamford, and Griffin (2018). Technology and the digital world can be wonderfully informative and formative, but we must make wise decisions. Time limits, learning how to discern truth from lies, and engaging in many helpful conversations can go a long way to helping young people develop healthy worldviews.

Questions

1. Approximately how many hours does your child spend engaging in social media? (Are you aware of your own media consumption?)
2. What are the issues in which you have found difficulty knowing what is true or not due to conflicting "expert" reports? Who do you trust to give you truth?
3. If it is difficult for us as adults to know what is true, how do we help our children navigate finding truth for themselves?
4. What are some non-negotiable truths for you? How do you pass them on to your children?

Conversations With Your Children

- What is truth?
- What are some issues where truth is essential for you?
- Who are some of the influencers you listen to on social media? What is it about them that you like? What kind of truths do they represent?
- How can social media be good? How can social media be bad?
- How many hours a day do you think you engage in social media?
- What happens to the world if there is "no truth"?

- Why are these words of Jesus so important: "I am the way and the truth and the life. No one comes to the Father except through me" (John 14:6).

The Voice of Culture

My friend, Dr. Walt Mueller, in his book *Youth Culture 101* writes:

> I like to think of culture as the "soup" in which our teenagers swim around and soak every day. The soup's ingredients include values, attitudes, and behaviors—as well as the media, peer group, language, and so on that express them. To know kids, we must lift the lid on the soup pot and see what's in the mix" (Mueller, 2007, p. 35).

As young people engage in the "soup pot" of culture, there are many more voices that are influencing their worldviews and perspectives. With the advent of social media, more ingredients are being added to the soup. If I could make an overarching statement about this entire book, it would be this: We need more adults jumping into the soup mix with our children and youth! This needs to happen by adults, children, and teenagers engaging in intentional conversations, sharing meals, and taking an interest in the various ingredients in the soup pot. Culture is not something that should passively happen.

Culture is comprised of beliefs, clothing, food, language, music, stories, communication, traditions, and many more aspects of life in society. We begin to see the development of nations and other cultures beginning in Genesis 10 and, shortly after in Genesis 11, we see the positive and the negative aspects of culture. In Genesis 11:1–4, we see that the people living on the plains of Shinar (Babylonia) were able to work together and create. In fact, in Genesis 11:6, God says within the Holy Trinity, "The LORD said, 'If as one people speaking the same language they have begun to do this, then nothing they plan to do will be impossible for them.'" What an amazing and often overlooked statement! When people are unified and come together, "nothing they plan to do will be impossible for them"! Here is the problem found in verse 4b: "so that we may make a name for ourselves."

Culture is a gift given to us by God. Think of your favorite food, music, traditions, and even clothing. In fact, God is the very first clothing fashion designer (See Genesis 3:21). These elements of culture can bring a level of joy when we enjoy them and when engaged in properly. Every good gift is given to us by God and we should thank God and proclaim His great name. Instead of this, we seek to make a name for ourselves with those gifts. This is a problem. The culture that brought people together on the plains of Shinar became corrupted due to their own selfish desire to make a name for themselves. Young people are also tempted to make a name for themselves. (Remember our cautionary tale of Steven Fernandez?)

Ironically, I see the same behaviors in adults. How many ministry leaders have worked harder to make a name for themselves rather than proclaiming the name of God? My goal as a ministry leader has never been to become popular or famous. Even in my teaching, speaking, and writing, I have fears about becoming *well-known*. Even as I write this book, I don't care if people remember my name. Instead, I want them to recognize that God needs them to help young people discern through the many voices in their lives. I hope God is glorified and the principles help bring youth and families closer to Christ.

When I was younger, God was doing some amazing things through our ministry, and He allowed me to be a part of those things. As I was able to start speaking in a variety of places, people wanted to become friends. I am a "people person" so I love making friends. However, I noticed that some people wanted to get to know me so I could help them with their platform. I don't have a problem with this. In fact, at the time of this writing, I host a podcast with some well-known youth ministry professionals through the Association of Youth Ministry Educators, and I love promoting people and their work. My goal is to connect youth ministry academics with youth ministry practitioners. However, back then when people wanted to befriend me, I discovered that it was because they wanted to make a name for themselves or their ministry. Shouldn't all of us be more focused on proclaiming God? Don't get me wrong, I want this book to become very well-received and have many copies being read around the country and world. More than that I want the message of this book to proclaim the goodness of God in the lives of young people and their families.

Make no mistake: churches and ministries create a culture. Youth ministries create a culture. Our homes have a culture. In fact, every organization we find ourselves involved with has a culture. *Digital cultural existence* is another significant place that creates and distorts culture. Young people desire to be loved and accepted so much that they blur who they really are with their digital persona. The question we need to ask is, "Does this culture glorify God and proclaim *His* name?" I encourage all of us, as committed disciples of Jesus, to ask hard questions like,

- "Is my church (or pastor/youth pastor) focused on proclaiming God or making a name for themselves?"
- "Am I the center of attention or do I make God the center of attention?" Another related question is, "Am I making my children the center of my attention or am I making God the center of my attention?"
- "Am I trying to make a name for myself at work or do I want to glorify God—no matter the cost?"
- "What kind of culture am I creating at home for my family?"
- "How can I be intentional about what is going on in culture in order to have *God-driven* conversations with my children?"
- "How am I guiding my child, grandchild, or mentor into proclaiming God rather than themselves?"

As a natural part of individuation, it is not uncommon for young people to have created multiple selves (Clark, 2011) as they begin to explore their identity outside their family structure. This is especially true when it comes to social media presences, each social media platform offering the ability to portray many more different *selves*. While self-discovery is a normal process of identity formation, social media allows for the creation of significantly more "multiple selves" as a world of new perspectives are open to young people. Social media is another way our children and youth are learning to navigate a culture with a variety of individual and disconnected voices in their lives. Further, young people are blurring the lines between the Christian faith, and other faiths as well as religious and spiritual practices. This is another type of "Third Culture Kid" as Jeff Keuss would say in his book appropriately titled, *Blur: A New Paradigm for Understanding Youth Culture*.

Too many conflicting voices can be confusing to us. Along with this thought, too many different cultivated personalities can cause confusion as well and hinders identity formation. It is one thing to take a while to process who we are, it is another thing to put on too many false faces that hinder us from deciding who we want to become. At some point, we as adults need to guide our children to their true north. We need to help them solidify a worldview that is going to serve as a compass for them so they are not, as the Apostle Paul says, "tossed back and forth by the waves, and blown here and there by every wind of teaching and by the cunning and craftiness of people in their deceitful scheming" (Ephesians 4:14).

While I am a proponent of diversity, there are just some things that do not belong in the cultural soup of our children and youth. Imagine making a savory beef and vegetable soup and adding a cup of sugar! In developing a coherent, practical worldview to live by, we must also teach our children and youth to be discerning about cultural elements. At one point, our culture had legalized slavery. Just because a culture says something is legally okay, that does not automatically make it morally okay. Our moral values come from God's Word, not from cultural zeitgeist (spirit of the time). This is exactly why Scripture tells us that the truth of God's Word does not change though culture may (Isaiah 40:8).

My sons and I have an interesting way of engaging in the cultures of other countries. For the past 14 years, we have sponsored a child in Nicaragua named Ludy through Compassion International. We have sponsored Ludy since he was four years old. We are now sponsoring our second child, Nilson. The ministry of Compassion International allows families to provide education, nutrition, medication, and spiritual nurture. It has been fun getting to know Ludy and the culture of Nicaragua through the eyes of Ludy by exchanging letters, celebrating Ludy's birthdays and holidays, and hearing about the impact of his school and Compassion International. My kids have the opportunity to write to these children as well but the awesome part is when we get a letter back from Ludy or Nilson. We get to experience the unique parts of their culture without having to travel to Nicaragua. It is a beautiful thing to see these children grow up and see the world through their eyes. I am thankful for organizations such as Compassion International to be a voice in the lives of so many children!

My encouragement to you and your family is to look a little deeper into the culture in which you live. What are the things that are unique that you and your family can celebrate? How can you expose your children to other healthy elements of your culture? Intentionally looking at the beneficial, as well as negative, elements of culture can help expand your child's worldview. For instance, it is wonderful to know on any given Sunday, the cultural and spiritual practice of the Lord's Supper is celebrated by believers in millions of churches. No matter how it is practiced, the meaning of Christ's life, sacrifice, resurrection, and ascension through the Lord's Supper draws the body of Christ around the world together!

Any cultural practices that glorify God are always good. Remember, God is the giver of culture and it is our role to help our children and youth see the elements of culture that are good and celebrate them. On the other hand, like anything else, we need to be intentional about evaluating what elements are helpful and which are not.

Time: We all engage in culture and, most of the time, we are not aware of it. It is sort of like being a fish and having no awareness that you are surrounded by water. We take in our culture with very little discernment. Since we spend so much time surrounded by culture, we need to learn to be intentional about what we take in. For instance, music is a cultural element. As we know, some music can be beneficial and some music can send destructive messages. As adults who love our children and youth, it is our responsibility to spend our time evaluating the helpful or harmful elements of culture. This, of course, takes time.

Transparency: Culture is not necessarily something that is or isn't transparent. Culture simply *is*. However, culture comes with assumptions that we may or may not be aware of. For instance, some cultures are much more honoring of their elders than others. We may not be aware of this until we see things done differently in another culture. Eastern culture has a higher value on the wisdom of the elderly. Western cultures are not as focused in this area. We can certainly learn from Eastern culture. The only way we will see the transparency of culture is to spend a significant amount of time critically engaging in culture. In other words, we need to be more cautious about music, movies, shows, messages, etc. that we engage or consume.

Trust: Can we trust the elements of a secular culture? It is difficult to trust clothing, food, music entertainment, and the things that make up culture. Not all culture is *good*. Currently, Western culture is becoming increasingly secularized. While all truth is God's truth, not everything that claims to be truth is. Standards of dress, clothing, music, movies, and more must be looked at through a biblically-informed worldview to determine if it should be engaged in or not. This takes discernment. Paul had to address this with Gentiles who became believers. Were new Gentile converts expected to participate in all the Jewish customs like circumcision? No. In fact, Gentiles were told, "As for the Gentile believers, we have written to them our decision that they should abstain from food sacrificed to idols, from blood, from meat of strangled animals and from sexual immorality" (Acts 21:25).

Our culture has become hypersexualized. One of my favorite apologists is C. S. Lewis. Approximately twenty years before the sexual revolution of the 1960s, C. S. Lewis wrote how sexuality had gotten in such a mess.[11] A popular theory was that people did not talk enough about sexuality—as if it were something to be ashamed of. Lewis contended that even as people began talking more and more about sex, sexuality had become even more of a mess. Lewis argued if not talking about sex caused sexuality to become messed up, then talking about it more should have been the cure. The problem is, the more people talked about sex, the more messed up it has become! That Lewis was warning about this "slippery slope" in the 1940s and 1950s before the sexual revolution only magnifies how distorted sexuality has become today! Not only are people talking about all types of "abnormal" sexual practices, but immoral sexuality is proliferated in all sorts of media such as television, movies, social media, and more!

Lewis went on to point out that sexuality, like our appetite for food, is nothing to be ashamed of. He was right of course, unless a person's sexual or physical appetites are unsatiable. To be hungry is one thing, but to drool every time someone sees a picture of food is another. There is a right way and a wrong way to view the gift of sexuality that God gave us. The right way, of course, is in a holy, heterosexual, God-ordained marriage that practices fidelity and allegiance to God's precepts on sexuality. All other ways are akin to a gluttonous person

---

[11] Lewis, C. S. (1952). *Mere Christianity*. Macmillan Publishers. New York.

salivating over the smallest morsel of food after having had a five-course meal! In my years as a youth pastor, to even talk about God-ordained sexuality was quite risky with students since some parents rarely, if ever, talked about God-ordained sexuality. It is as if we have allowed the world to shame us into not talking about sex with our children because it has become filthy. However it is the world that has strayed from healthy sexuality. As Christians who care about our young, we should be the first to talk about God-ordained, healthy sexuality. If we do not, the world will show our children and youth filth and claim it as "normal"!

Anyone who has been around since the 1960s can see the slippery slope that the sexual revolution has gone down. It seems there are fewer and fewer sexual taboos in our culture. Children are being sexualized in a way that we are not often aware of. There are films like, *Call Me By Your Name, For A Lost Soldier, L.I.E., Cuties,* and an increasing number of films showing the sexualization of children. Music has become incredibly sexualized. A variety of television shows are now showing not only explicit heterosexual acts but homosexual acts as well. We are now seeing shows that are showing heterosexual and homosexual acts among teens. Our increasingly secular culture is becoming an *anything-goes,* sexual culture. Even though God gave the gift of sex, humanity continues to distort it. Instead of sex being seen as an act that builds trust, intimacy, and binding couples together, sex is now used as recreation.

One of the most abused drugs on college campuses is sildenafil citrate, better known to others as Viagra (Atsbeha, et. al., 2021). It is speculated that the reason college-age students are abusing sildenafil citrate is due to the proliferation and accessibility of pornography. When being exposed to, and engaging with pornography, young adults are having difficulty performing sexually with a real person. Unfortunately, sexuality continues to lose the sacred aspects God intended. Of course, this is bound to happen when we take a great gift and abuse it. Sexuality is probably the most divisive voice in our culture today. It is divisive because our culture continues to push sexuality without limits. Wise voices are needed to speak into the life of our children and youth!

I would not be surprised if other sexual taboos continue to become normal in our culture. We will see sexual deviants continuing to go after our children and youth in much more nefarious ways. It is not possible to completely shelter our children from the secular culture. One tool we can use to protect our children is to have age-appropriate and biblically-based conversations with them. More than conversations (as C. S. Lewis has alluded to), we need to help our children understand the emotional, spiritual, and even physical damage sex outside of marriage can cause. When it comes to sexuality, the voice of wisdom must prevail. If you are uncomfortable having these types of conversations with your children, it may be appropriate to invite mentors to join in those conversations with you.

Questions

1. What are the unique elements of your culture that you celebrate with your children?
2. What traditions do you celebrate that can be handed down from generation to generation?
3. What favorite cultural elements do you enjoy (types of music, food, holiday celebrations, etc.)?

4. How do you expose your children to different cultures that are healthy?
5. What potentially unhealthy cultures do you or your child participate in?
6. What cultural elements might you participate in that you need to become more aware of?
7. How are you engaging in age-appropriate and biblically-based conversations about sexuality?

Conversations With Your Children

- What would be a fun way for us to engage in another culture?
- How can elements of culture (music, food, clothing, movies, etc.) be good? How can they be harmful?
- What are some family celebrations or traditions you love participating in? What are some of those things you would like to pass on to your children?

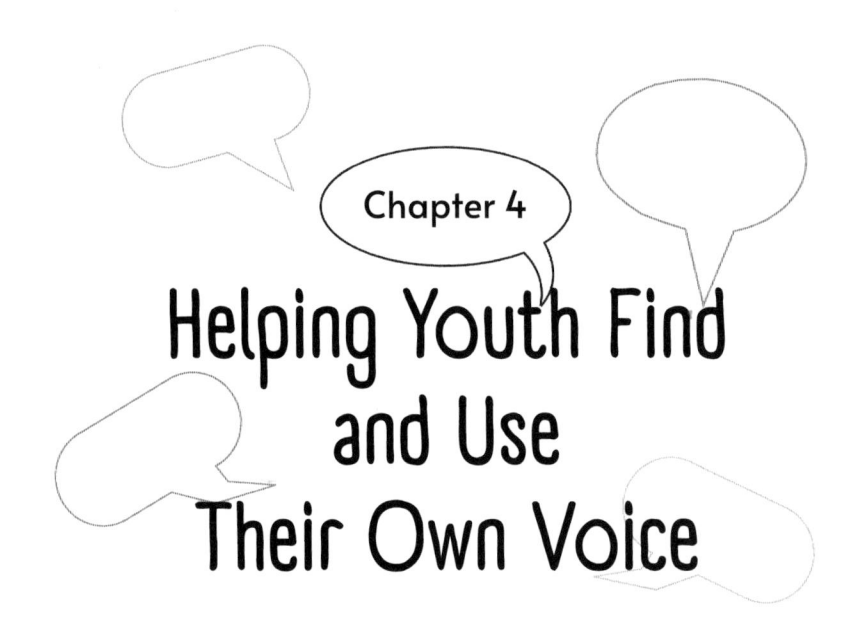

Chapter 4
Helping Youth Find and Use Their Own Voice

This section is written for children whose parents are not trusted voices. I wish all parents or grandparents deeply loved their children. Unfortunately, my experience and research shows this is not the case. In fact, there seems to be an increasing number of young people who feel abandoned and unloved. This is heartbreaking. With this in mind, I am going to write the final part in a different type of voice. While you read it as a nurturing adult involved in the lives of young people, I want you to be able to have your voice use my voice. I hope the following words will help children and youth find their own voice. So, here it goes:

To all my young friends: Let's talk about the challenge of having neglectful parents or a culture that has abandoned them. First, let me say, "I am sorry. That is not the way God intended it." To say my parents were less than perfect is an understatement. However, going through the steps I am about to share helped me to forgive them and we developed a much better and healthier relationship. All three of my adopted sons came from homes with extremely horrible parents. They faced abuse, neglect, distrust, trauma, and all sorts of terrible things that have taken them years to overcome. All three of my sons entered my life when they were older (around ages 10 and 11). Honestly, they have come a long way, but they still have some ways to go. The best advice I can give myself, you, and them is this:

1. Have someone to talk to.
2. Learn to forgive. (You don't have to forget.)
3. Seek counseling.
4. Learn from the mistakes of others and avoid them.
5. If you have good parents, make sure to thank them! (It will mean more than you know!)

Have someone to talk to.

Unhealthy people keep harmful secrets. Unhealthy people have unwritten rules: Don't tell. Don't ask. Don't feel. If a child is abused, the child is warned by an adult not to tell anyone. In fact, many adult abusers threaten abused children that if they tell anyone, horrible things will happen to them or their loved ones. Abuse is a terrible and painful secret. Children who are abused never get to ask why they are being treated the way they are. Abused children often must ignore their pain and feelings. They stuff down their feelings. All these rules are very unhealthy. It is for this reason that you must speak to an adult you can trust. A teacher, a coach, a youth pastor… someone. You should also know that these folks are the ones who are typically trained to walk through this situation with you. Trusted adults are some of the healthy voices you want, and need, to listen to. The difficult challenge may be believing there are healthy adults who want the best for you. If you have struggled with an unhealthy family, it is difficult to believe any other adult can have your best interests in mind.

Learn to forgive. (You don't have to forget.)

For all my children (and myself), learning to forgive has been a very difficult journey. You should note that I have called it a journey because it takes time and does not happen overnight. However, forgiveness allows the one who forgives a sense of being released from bondage. Jesus said in Matthew 16:19, "I will give you the keys of the kingdom of heaven; whatever you bind on earth will be bound in heaven, and whatever you loose on earth will be loosed in heaven." In the long run, if you do not forgive a person who harmed you, ultimately you are giving them control over your life emotionally because of the anger, bitterness, and harmful thoughts you may have against them. Forgiving does not mean you must forget. Forgetting would be harmful because we would possibly repeat the same mistakes as those who harmed us.

On a different note, have you ever wondered why God doesn't only forgive you for your mistakes but also does not remember them—at all—ever? Psalm 103:11–12 says, "For as high as the heavens are above the earth, so great is his love for those who fear him; as far as the east is from the west, so far has he removed our transgressions from us." Along with 1 John 1:8–9, "If we claim to be without sin, we deceive ourselves and the truth is not in us. If we confess our sins, he is faithful and just and will forgive us our sins and purify us from all unrighteousness," we can be assured God does not hold our wrongdoings against us. Here is the other reason God can forget our sins: He has nothing to learn from them! Being all-knowing, God does not need to learn anything from the mistakes of human beings. We do need to learn from our mistakes so we don't repeat them.

Here is the kicker though: If we are going to be God's children, then we must become like our "Abba" (Daddy). We must follow in His footsteps to forgive. Just as God has set us free from our mistakes, we can move on in our healing by forgiving other people of their mistakes. This applies whether, on a scale of 1 to 10, you have a 1 or a 9 for parents! I know it is not easy if your parents were a 1. My sons know it was not easy either, but they have made great progress concerning their biological parents and I have seen it set them free emotionally!

Seek Counseling.

Due to my poor upbringing, I did not realize how angry I was at my parents. Sometimes children grow up in homes where abuse, neglect, or other harmful behaviors are thought of as normal. It's all they know and have not had better examples. When children get older and see other families or understand their family was unhealthy, they can become very angry. (This was me.) I felt like I had to keep doing so good that I would eventually *earn* the love and approval of my parents. This can be confusing even if your parents are a 9. Your parents may push you to do well because they care for you and want the best for you. Unfortunately, this pushing can feel painful. On the other hand, sometimes we need to be pushed by trusted voices to do things we would not want to do.

Getting counseling should be seen as a normal part of life. Proverbs 15:22 says, "Plans fail for lack of counsel, but with many advisers they succeed." Smart people recognize the need for counselors in their life. We have school counselors who guide us in academics. Pastors serve as counselors. In fact, smart people often get pre-marital counseling from pastors to help them start married life on the right foot. Why is it then that people have a difficult time seeking counseling? Sometimes it is pride. Sometimes it is pain. Sometimes we have been taught to *keep the secret*. Whatever the reason, people may need help getting counseling. It is the second step to healing. The first step is recognizing the need to be honest. The wisdom we can gain from counselors can also become trusted voices to listen to.

Learn from the mistakes of others and avoid them.

The most successful people are not the ones who succeed all the time. They have made many mistakes, but the key is they learned from their mistakes and they learn from the mistakes of others. The mistakes of others and our own mistakes do not have to ruin us. In fact, mistakes can provide great direction and success—if we learn and grow from them.

If you have good parents, make sure to thank them!

Sometimes becoming a teenager, as you seek to establish your identity—to become your own person—and grow in wisdom, there can be a challenge because your parents did such a good job raising you. When this happens and struggles come your way, you might be reluctant to tell your parents some of your struggles for fear of disappointing them or maybe you might be embarrassed. This is understandable. I have three sons adopted "out of the system." I know that some young people just have bad parents. It pains me to say that. Regardless, even at my age, I still need, and have, mentors.

Here is the thing: Even though I spent a lot of years as a youth pastor (and now a professor and a pastor), I still want my sons to have wise people speak into their lives. I am not sure where my sons would rank me on the scale of "bad to good" parenting (I hope I am not a 2 or 3, but I know I am not a 9 or 10.) Also, I need other adults to be in a relationship with my sons because I don't have all the knowledge and wisdom in the world! What I am saying here is, no matter what type of parents you had, everyone needs a good mentor or two in their lives.

Ways to Discover Your Voice

The way we go about seeking to discover who we are and how we can gain a voice that speaks up for ourselves and helps others begins with solitude and meditation, then community, and then finding our passion. When we find our passion, we then find our purpose. Our purpose in life is what helps us gain a voice and becomes part of our identity. Unfortunately, many people go about this process in reverse. Many people struggle to know their purpose in life because their passions frequently shift. This happens because our passions are driven by a desire to belong and be in community—even if the community is unhealthy. It is when life becomes desperate that people then turn to God. In fact, many people become so dissatisfied with life that they blame God when He was the last person they turned to.

To have a life of purpose, we must first learn to listen to God through solitude and meditation. When we do this, we gain confidence in our lives. When we have been strengthened by God, we will seek the right community that will help us gain a passion for the things God is passionate about. When you become passionate about the things God is passionate about, you then have purpose and direction. All through this process, you are discovering more about who you and God are.

Solitude & Meditation

If you really want to know who you are, you must be willing to be still and quiet in order to hear the still small voice of God that is the whisper in your soul. It is my hope and prayer that you not only believe in God, but you have a personal relationship with the One who created you and knows you better than you know yourself. Taking time to be quiet and reflect on your identity allows you to gain confidence in who you are becoming. There is a big difference between being lonely and seeking solitude. Many influential people spent time in solitude to drown out all the chaotic and conflicting voices in their lives and rid themselves of anxiety. Moses, King David, Jesus, St. Patrick, St. Benedict, Dr. Martin Luther King, Jr., and many others have benefited from times of solitude, prayer, and meditation.

The list of ancient and modern individuals who participated in solitude and prayer is innumerable, and yet, in our current busy Western mindset, it seems that solitude, meditation, and prayer have been very limited. It is no secret that Dr. Martin Luther King, Jr., was steeled by his prayer and meditation life. Dr. King often received death threats and, at times, was very tempted to give up leadership in the civil rights movement. Dr. King accomplished great things because he knew that his strength came from God.

It is no wonder there is so much anxiety in our lives. Solitude and meditation are the very ways that God speaks into our souls. If you want to discover your own identity and your voice, you must be able to be still and listen to God who created you. Solitude and meditation allow us to calm the noise in our heads. Frankly, this takes some practice. When most of my students begin habits of prayer and meditation they get very distracted. That is normal when one begins practicing spiritual disciplines like these.

Participating in solitude and meditation is sort of like doing weight training for the first time. At first, you are not very strong and after a couple of days, your muscles hurt. This is because you have not used them in this way before. However, the more you keep at the weight training, and use the right weights with the right techniques, it is not too long before you see improvement. Since many people are not used to solitude and biblical meditation, it takes some time to improve. Having one or two Scriptures to meditate on can be very helpful. After your mind and spirit have begun to calm, you can listen for the quiet voice of God. It is amazing how much peace you can discover through solitude and meditation. There are entire books written on the subject of Christian spiritual formation practices, including meditation. I encourage you to read more on this topic.[12]

Community

Human beings were created for community. No one can do well with continued solitude. While community is a good thing, we must also be careful to be in the right community. If a group of individuals is not looking out for what is truly best for us, we are probably not in the right community. A healthy

---

[12] Valuable spiritual formation books include the following: *Celebration of Discipline: The Path to Spiritual Growth* by Richard Foster, *Invitation to a Journey* by M. Robert Mulholland, *The Spirit of Disciplines* by Dallas Willard, and finally, *Invitation to Solitude and Silence: Experiencing God's Transforming Presence* by Ruth Haley Barton.

community encourages healthy choices. A community that is concerned about your health is going to send you the right messages. For instance, I assume that most Americans know the dangers and health issues of smoking, and yet, people still choose to smoke. It becomes an addiction that negatively affects their health and their lives in the long run. I cannot begin to imagine the number of teens who, despite knowing the dangers of smoking and being warned about it by the adult community, decide to smoke anyway to please a community of their peers who smoke. Here is a very simple fact: Healthy communities produce healthy individuals.

Everyone needs a community of people who will be their cheerleaders. However, these cheerleaders do not only cheer for you when things are going great; they also cheer for you when things get tough! While we may not like it when somebody tells us we have done something wrong, they are trying to keep us from making bigger mistakes so we can fully live the passionate and purposeful life God has called us to participate in. I cannot think of anything sadder than a person who lives life without passion and purpose and then without cheerleaders to help encourage them. I cannot imagine how much more difficult the life of Dr. King would have been had he not had a community around him that supported his passion and purpose. Remember, we need to seek God's input first and this will help us to more easily discover what community of people is the most beneficial for us.

Passion

As we get older, we begin to discover the things we are passionate about. There is a big difference between being passionate about a certain toy when you are five years old and being passionate about stopping human trafficking when you are sixteen years old or older! Usually what happens is, as you get older, you get more exposed to many more things that go on in the world. There is a lot of beauty and things to be enjoyed in this life, but there are also a lot of things that break God's heart. Poverty, injustice, human trafficking, oppression… there are plenty of causes out there to get involved in. However, tackling these things can be extremely difficult. It is even more difficult if we are alone and we do not get our wisdom from God and others.

When God gives you a passion for something, it is because He is equipping you to be a difference-maker. As much as a secular culture wants to do away with God, can you imagine where the Civil Rights Movement would be today if God had not raised up a person like Dr. Martin Luther King, Jr.? This great man was a pastor who listened to God and was strengthened by people who were passionate about the same things Dr. King was passionate about. It is for these reasons God gave Dr. King a call, a community, and then lit a passion in Dr. King's life. No doubt, Dr. King's purpose was made evident through the elements of prayer, meditation, community, and passion.

Purpose

Purpose not only gives us direction, but it also gives us meaning in life. Dr. King's purpose in life was that of moving Civil Rights forward. Dr. King did so at great cost to his family and his own life, yet he had found a purpose he was willing to die for. I am a believer that you do not know how to live until you find something you are willing to die for. It is passion and purpose that give us a mission in life. Here is the thing however: remember I mentioned that Dr. King was tempted to walk away from leadership in the Civil Rights Movement, but he could not because he heard the voice of God tell him to take a stand for justice! If Dr. King had gone about this mission backward, he would have missed the voice of God calling him to his purpose. Further, it is the voice of God and His encouragement that keeps us going when things get tough. Dr. King was a testimony to this.

I should also point out something that is very important. Dr. King gained his approach to non-violence by studying the life and the teachings of Jesus Christ. Dr. King was a Christian pastor who heard from God, clearly surrounded himself with an encouraging community, clearly felt a passion, and lived his purpose.

Questions

1. How anxious are you about the future?
2. How do you deal with anxiety or concerns?
3. What adult do you have in your life that will listen to you, no matter what?
4. How do you listen for the voice of God in your life? How do you know if He has spoken to you?
5. What questions do you have about either talking to or listening to God?
6. If you do hear from God, how do you act upon what God reveals to you?
7. How can your community help you hear from God?
8. What type of community do you surround yourself with? Does this community make wise choices or poor choices?
9. Do you listen to the voices of wise people in your healthy community?

10. What are you passionate about? Another way to think about this is, how do you want to make a difference with your life? Are you still discovering your passion?

11. How can the right community help you live your passion? How can the wrong community keep you from living your passion?

12. What do you think your purpose in life might be? Are you still discovering that purpose?

13. What are some things you wish someone would tell you more about so you can understand better?

Appendix

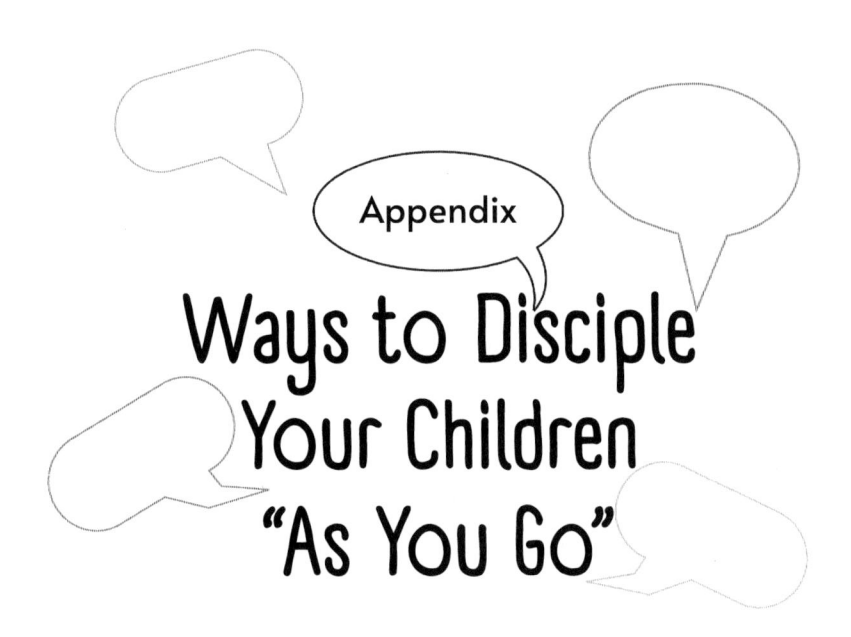

Ways to Disciple Your Children "As You Go"

Discipleship should not be something scary or time-consuming. In fact, when we consider Deuteronomy 6, much of discipleship is "as you go," or as you do life together. Deuteronomy 6:7–9 says,

> Impress [the commandments of God in His Word] on your children. Talk about [His Word] when you sit at home and when you walk along the road, when you lie down and when you get up. Tie [God's commandments] as symbols on your hands and bind them on your foreheads. Write them on the doorframes of your houses and on your gates.

Notice these verses imply an "as you go" way of discipleship with your children. Further, these guiding statements are both for the home and the community as indicated by the doorframes and gates.

Discipleship and theology are simply speaking about the things of God and how His Word applies to our lives. Don't worry about your kids knowing more than you do or asking hard questions. Discovering answers together is, in and of itself, discipleship.

It is also important to remember to do things that are simple, functional, and sustainable. Here are some ideas:

At Home

- **Read through the Psalms.** My son and I drive together to his school and my work. We work our way through the book of Psalms, one psalm each morning. He will read the psalm aloud and then we discuss what he thinks about what is written and how we can apply it to our lives. The Psalms allow us to find our comfort in God, but they also allow us to see that it is okay to have a whole range of emotions we can express toward God. As we finish, either he or I pray. You can also mix it up by doing the same thing with Proverbs or the Gospel of John.
- **Develop a Family Mission Statement.** My family's mission statement is to "Love God, Love each other, Love others, and relieve suffering whenever and wherever possible in the name of Jesus." We then try to go out several times a year and join in some sort of local community mission work. This is something you can include in your Family Video Prayer Journal and Family Connections Group.
- **Learn about spiritual disciplines and put them into practice.** Solitude, fasting, giving, prayer, being present, study, etc. For instance, when children are old-

er, teach them to fast from electronics or even food for a short time. Talk to them about the discipline of giving and use periods of the year (Christmas, birthdays, Thanksgiving, etc.) and encourage them to think about how the family can give to others.

- **Practice active listening.** As parents, we spend a lot of time teaching, correcting, and disciplining. It comes with the job. However, we need to set a time apart, at least once a week, to just listen to our kids. This means no distractions. Put the phone away. Listen to listen, not answer. Look your child in the eyes. Lean forward. Really LISTEN. Repeat back what they are saying. "I think what I hear you saying is _____. Is that correct?" This lets your child know you are listening. Ask simple questions like: "How do you see God at work in your life?" or "How is God helping you through this tough time?"

- **Pray with intention.** Find a time each day when intentional prayer (not the rote mealtime prayers) can be expressed together.

- **Create a Family Video Prayer Journal.** Record your challenges (prayers) and hope (praises). Keep these in a video file. Save them to the cloud (or have individual flash drives for each month) and after six months or so, go back and review your videos and see how God has moved. Do this as a family so as your kids get older, they will remember, and have access to, the legacy of valuing prayer in your family.

- **Have each family member choose a life verse.** Discuss and memorize these verses together.

- **Look for teachable moments.** The best ones occur naturally. Whether it comes from a movie, a song, or seeing somebody do something, use those as times to engage in conversation and ask your child, "What do you think about that?" "What do you think God would say about it?"
- **Do a regular family game night or something else special.** You can have great conversations as you play a game or just go out for ice cream. Take time to be present with your children intentionally, and have fun.

In Church and Your Community

- **Attend worship together.** This sounds simple, but the modern Western church is too segregated by ages. Children from at least 4th grade can learn to worship. Prior to the service, challenge your child to listen for at least one thing they can learn. After the service, compare what you and your child learned and talk about it. Research shows that many young people leave the faith in their later teens because there is not enough intergenerational interaction.
- **Form family connections groups.** Be intentional about creating and connecting with church family affinity groups. It is amazing the amount of support you get from each other! Be intentional about planning a quarterly get-together. Maybe it is a picnic, a cookout, or meeting at Dairy Queen. A game night also works well! Invite "adopted" singles, grandparents, aunts, and uncles, etc. These groups can be seasonal, some-

thing that happens during the summer or a couple of weeks during the school year.

- **Serve in a ministry area together at your church.** Whether it is singing, running AV, greeting, taking up the offering, serving in children's ministry... whatever it is, this is how you train up the next generation of leaders by teaching them to serve alongside adults. Youth are the church now, not just of the future, and if we do not engage them now through owning ministry, they will not be around to be "the church of the future."

- **Find a spiritual mentor for your child outside the home.** The earlier you do this, the better because your child will come to a point in their lives where they will have situations they do not want to talk to you about, either because they are embarrassed or they do not want to disappoint you.

- **Surround your child with other godly adults.** This can be a youth leader, coach, teacher, "adoptive" grandparents, aunts and uncles, etc. The fact is that the more Christian, caring adults you have involved in different capacities, your child will be surrounded by Christian nurture. People often freak out if you ask them to mentor a child because they think they are not equipped, so I use the term "spiritual encourager." My son has a spiritual grandma named Ms. Harriett. Jamie will go over and help with yard work or other tasks and Ms. Harriett takes time to play games, teach Jamie how to cook or bake, and most importantly, listen to him. God intends for the entire community to nurture and spiritually guide our young people.

As you can see, discipleship does not have to be difficult. You don't need to be a Bible scholar to disciple your children. My sons and I have often learned deeper spiritual concepts together. By listening to them process God's Word as we go, I learn a great deal from my kids, making me a better parent, pastor, and professor.

Having more natural spiritual conversations with my sons allows me to point them to Jesus Christ every day. In Him, we are free to do the things that work for our family. We don't have to do them perfectly, because His righteousness covers our sins and shortcomings. Following the guidance of His Spirit, you will establish rhythms that work for your family.

Works Cited

Atsbeha, B. W., Kebede, B. T., Birhanu, B. S., Yimenu, D. K., Belay, W. S., & Demeke, C. A. (2021). The weekend drug; recreational use of sildenafil citrate and concomitant factors: A cross-sectional study. *Frontiers in Medicine, 8*. https://doi.org/10.3389/fmed.2021.665247.

Bernstein, N. (2014). *Burning down the house: The end of juvenile prison*. The New Press. New York.

Best, S. (2014). Agency and structure in Zygmunt Bauman's modernity and the Holocaust. *Irish Journal of Sociology, 22*(1), 67–87. https://doi-org.fuller.idm.oclc.org/10.7227/IJS.22.1.5.

Chapman, G. and Pellicane, A (2020). *Screen kids: 5 relational skills every child needs in a tech-driven world*. Northfield Publishing. Chicago.

Bonhoeffer, D. (1995). *The cost of discipleship*. Touchstone. New York.

Clark, C. (2011). *Hurt 2.0: Inside the world of today's teenagers.* Baker Academic. Grand Rapids, MI.

Conti, A. (2017, April 13). *How Baby Scumbag's quest for social media fame ended in disaster.* VICE. Retrieved from https://www.vice.com/en/article/wdbg5w/how-baby-scumbags-quest-for-social-media-fame-ended-in-disaster.

DeVries, M. (2004) *Family-based youth ministry.* Intervarsity Press. Downers Grove, IL.

DeVries, M. (2008). *Sustainable youth ministry: Why most youth ministry doesn't last and what your church can do about it.* IVP Books. Chicago.

Elkind, D. (1981). *The hurried child: Growing up too fast too soon.* Da Capo Press. Lebanon, IN.

Erikson, E. H. (1950; 1963). *Childhood and society.* W. W. Norton. New York.

Fallesen, P., & Gähler, M. (2020). Family type and parents' time with children: longitudinal evidence for Denmark. *Acta Sociologica,* 63(4), 361–380. https://doi.org/10.1177/0001699319868522.

FAQ About the Hmong. Hmong American Center. Retrieved from https://www.hmongamericancenter.org/faq.

Forman-Hoffman, V. L. and Cunningham, C. L. (2008). Geographical clustering of eating disordered behaviors in U.S. high school students. *Int. J. Eat. Disord.,* 41: 209–214. https://doi.org/10.1002/eat.20491.

Foster, Richard J. (1998). *Celebration of discipline: The path of spiritual growth.* Harper Collins. San Francisco.

Glanville, M. (2012). *Jesus ate his way through the gospels - eaten with a tax-collector recently?* Retrieved from https://

www.markglanville.org/blog/2012/07/20/jesus-ate-his-way-through-the-gospels-eaten-with-a-tax-collector-recently.

Groppe, M. (2018). Pence defends faith as normal after TV host calls it crazy to think Jesus talks to him. *USA Today Online*. Retrieved from https://www.usatoday.com/story/news/politics/onpolitics/2018/02/19/pence-defends-faith-normal-after-tv-host-calls-crazy-think-jesus-talks-him/353088002/.

Hunter, R. (2021). *About me, about you*. Randall House. Nashville.

Keuss, J. (2014). *Blur: A new paradigm for understanding youth culture*. Zondervan. Grand Rapids.

Kegan, R. (1994). *In over our heads: The mental demands of modern life*. Harvard University Press. Cambridge.

Lewis, C. S. (1952). *Mere Christianity*. Macmillan Publishers. New York.

McDowell, A. (2018). Christian but not religious: Being church as Christian hardcore punk. *Sociology of Religion, 79*(1), 58–77. https://doi-org.fuller.idm.oclc.org/10.1093/socrel/srx033.

McGarry, M. (2019). *A biblical theology of youth ministry: Teenagers in the life of the church*. Randall House. Nashville.

McLeod, S. A. (2018, May 03). Erik Erikson's stages of psychosocial development. Simply Psychology. Retrieved from http://www.simplypsychology.org/Erik-Erikson.html.

Mueller, W. (2007). *Youth culture 101*. Youth Specialties. El Cajon.

Ortiz, P, Khin Khin, E. Traditional and new media's influence on suicidal behavior and contagion. *Behav Sci Law*. 2018; 36: 245–256. https://doi.org/10.1002/bsl.2338.

Ortiz-Ospina, E. (2020). Are parents spending less time with their kids? *Our World In Data*. Retrieved from https://ourworldindata.org/parents-time-with-kids.

Powell, K., Bamford A., Griffin, B. (2018). *Every parent's guide to navigating our digital world*. Fuller Youth Institute. Pasadena.

Sanchez, C.M. (2015, June 1). Teresa of Avila's "*The interior castle*" as an individualizing text. *Inquiries Journal Online*. Retrieved from http://www.inquiriesjournal.com/articles/1047/teresa-of-avilas-the-interior-castle-as-an-individualizing-text.

Smith, C. (2009). *Souls in transition: The religious & spiritual lives of emerging adults*. Oxford University Press. New York.

Smith, C., and Denton, M. L. (2005). *Soul searching: The religious and spiritual lives of American teenagers*. Oxford University Press. New York.

Willard, D. (1999). *The spirit of the disciplines: Understanding how God changes lives*. Harper One. San Francisco.